SHATTERED CEILING

Dearest Amruta,

love
Geet Mala Jalota
14/6/24

THE SHATTERED CEILING

Narratives of pioneering women

GEET MALA JALOTA

Anecdote
Publishing House
For the love of quality reading!

anecdotepublishinghouse.com
champreaders.com

Anecdote Publishing House
2nd Floor 2/15 Lane no. 2 Ansari Road,
Daryaganj-110002

Published by Anecdote Publishing House
Copyright © Geet Mala Jalota

First Edition 2024

ISBN 978-81-968952-8-0

MRP ₹ 350

All Rights Reserved.
No part of this publication may be reproduced, stored in a retrieval system, or transmitted in any form, or by any means — electronic, mechanical, photocopying, recording or otherwise — without the prior permission of the publisher. Opinions expressed in it are the author's own. The publisher is in no way responsible for these.

Book Promoted and Marketed by Champ Readers Pvt. Ltd.

Cover design by Rishikumar Thakur
Layout by Aaush Kumar
Printed by Thomson Press (India) Ltd, New Delhi

CONTENTS

Deena Mehta   1
First lady Trader and President of Bombay Stock Exchange

Sucheta Shah   18
Executive Director - Atlas Integrated Finance Ltd.

Vijayalakshmi Chabbra   36
The first lady Director General of Doordarshan (India) the world's largest Public Service Broadcaster

Anita Khurana   56
The first lady to be appointed as Commercial Director in Indian Airlines / Air India post-merger.

Panchali Upadhaya   76
VP Sales & Marketing - Herbalife, Among the first women directors in Flipkart

KRE'SHA Bajaj 90
Entrepreneur - Of the Love lehnga fame

Sushmita Chakraborty 110
Among the first few women professionals to reach Associate Director level position in IT Industry - CSC India

Kanika Saxena 132
1st lady to be Master Scuba Diving Trainer, VP Marketing Vodafone

Sanju Yadav 160
Marketing Head MSN Labs

Anuradha Deb 184
Founder - Process Work Institute of India, Coach, Therapist

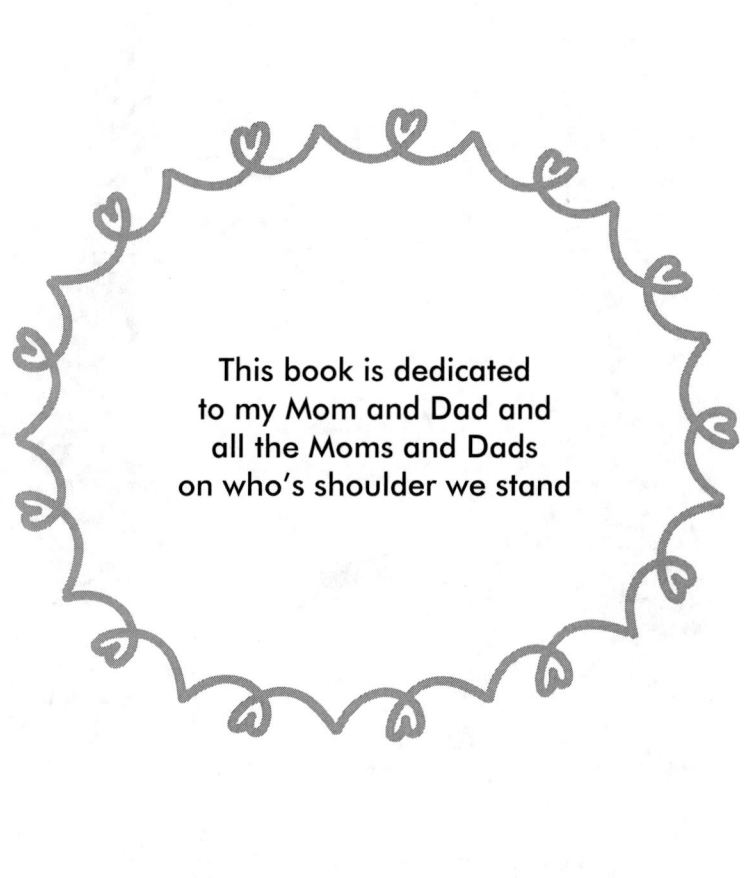

This book is dedicated
to my Mom and Dad and
all the Moms and Dads
on who's shoulder we stand

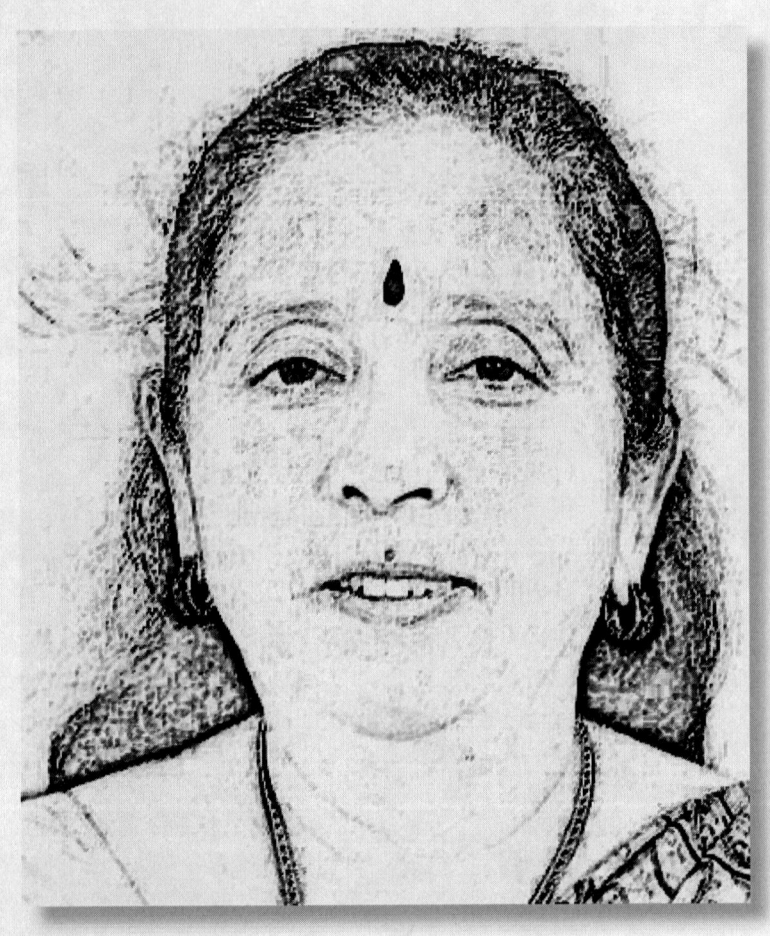

Deena Mehta BSE
FOUNDER AND MANAGING DIRECTOR, ACMIIL

AFTER 125 YEARS a woman dons the mantle of the President of the Bombay Stock Exchange. Of course, it speaks of her straight forward nature that she did not even realize that she was the first woman trader on the BSE floor, till somebody told her. It is only when you look at her achievements, you realize she is a force to be reckoned with. But when you talk to her, she has no airs. There is such an Indian-ness and wholesomeness about her no-nonsense speak that I think if she was to write an Indian version of Lean – In, it will become the Career Woman's almanac.

The promoter of Asit C. Mehta group of companies, Board member of Reliance Asset Reconstruction Company Ltd., Fino Bank and Gandhar Oil Refinery (India) Limited as an Independent Director. Advisor on educational Institutions Boards namely NMIMS Management School and Chairperson of NMIMS Alumni Association, IES Management Institute, Wilson College and MIT Pune.

❖ Former President of Bombay Stock Exchange, first woman Director on Board of BSE as well as the first woman President.

❖ Former director of National Payments Corporation of

India (NPCI).
- ❖ Promoter director of Central Depository Services Ltd as well as South Asian Federation of exchanges, the association of stock exchanges of SAARC countries.
- ❖ Invitee to International Securities Regulators Organization and a member of the Index Committee and Advisory Committee on mutual funds of stock exchange, Mumbai.
- ❖ Member of SEBI committees such as Review of Eligibility (CORE) norms of SEBI, Derivative Committee, Delisting Committee, Ethics Committee, and Investor Education.

She started her career with a Chartered Accountancy followed by a Masters in Management Studies (Finance) and also completed Fellow Member of Securities and Investment Institute London.

Mon, 1/3 10:19PM • 30:43
Can you walk us through your childhood days and maybe give a bit of your family background?
Originally, I come from a lower middle-class family. We are Gujaratis. For many years we were living in a chawl, then my parents moved to Borivali(W). That's how it has been. I mean, it might be very modest, but life hasn't been easy. My mother was a housewife, Initially, my father was in the tea business. Later on, he tried his luck as a builder. Finally, he settled down as an insurance agent.

Ours was more or less a joint family. My uncle stayed with us. We of course, visited other relatives very frequently. I used to go to my maternal uncle's place every vacation. We were very close to all our relatives. It was a close-knit family.

So, what was the atmosphere like at home? Was there any discrimination between girls and boys?
In my house it was *the* opposite. My father favored me more than my brother. He sent me to an English medium school and my brother was sent to a Gujarati medium school. Among my uncles' family too, I was the first daughter to be born in the family. There was no daughter in their families as all my uncles had sons only.

Didn't your mother protest, thinking that the girl might get spoilt?
No. nothing like that.

Who were you in school - The teacher's pet, the class bully or mouse or the back bencher?
Yes, I was a bookworm. I always stood second in my class, I never stood first because the girl who stood first was brilliant and she always did very well.

Apart from being a bookworm, did you take part in co-curricular activities? How did that shape you?
I was an all-rounder and liked to participate in sports and debates, competitions. I was also a very good organizer. I organized Navratri festivals, fun fairs etc. It made me a hyperactive person and gave me the extra edge, as far as boosting my confidence is concerned.

In fact, at the age of 17, I was selected to participate in an event called 'The Youth Voice', in Japan. I had the honour of being the first woman to be a part of this prestigious event.

It was a cultural exchange programme, where we were exposed to cultures of different countries. We travelled to Malaysia, from there onwards we went by ship all the way to Japan. In Japan we stayed with Japanese families and learnt about their culture, food habits, values and other practices.

What was the purpose of the trip?
It is more a goodwill kind of a thing. Some 50 international delegates from different countries participated, in addition to 500 Japanese participants. The essence of it was to bring about an understanding of different cultures and ideas.

It was my first venture abroad. Of course, in Junior College I had travelled across the country quite a bit. Then I got this opportunity to go to Japan. It was a big learning experience. I think it was really very fulfilling to be a part of this. Additionally, there were delegates from almost 50 countries, which made it even more thrilling It was an opportunity of a lifetime, to have been exposed to so many different cultures.

Where did you do your B Com and MMS from? And why MMS after CA?

I did MMS from NMIMS and B Com from Sydenham College after Chinai College.

Initially, my aim was to be an engineer but my father saw it as a profession for boys. Actually, at that point of time, I was not aware of the value and worth of IIT. If I had known, maybe I could have tried my luck there. The best option was to do CA. It was not a conscious decision; it was more by default. After having completed my B Com and CA, my college professor from Chinai joined as a professor of Management at NMIMS. He inspired us to join NMIMS. According to him MBA would be like a cherry topping on a cake. Thus, paying heed to his advice I left no stone unturned in preparing for the entrance exams. I was able to crack the entrance and thus got into MMS.

What was the MMS experience like?

MMS was pretty easy at that time because we had already done our CA. We found it relatively easier to study and to do what was required.

Was Crompton your first job? Somebody must have trained you professionally in your job?

Actually, learning is always done 'on the job'. There was nothing 'to teach'. In the initial days, I picked up the requisite skills just by being aware of my duties.

I was in the corporate office, which is at 1 VB Gandhi Marg as part of the corporate finance department. I was there from 1984 - 85. Mr. Nohria was our CEO at that point of time and Mr. Shetty was our Head of the department.

Why did you leave a secure job, where you had a nine to five schedule?
Job was secure but at the same time, I did not get job satisfaction. I felt that I could do much more than just a 'nine to five' job. I wanted more challenges in life, so I decided to switch jobs. Then after I had my first child, my husband suggested that I quit the job and try to do some business. My husband was a member of the Bombay Stock Exchange. So, that is how I joined the exchange and got into stock broking. Actually I started the firm and my husband joined me subsequently.

Did you feel scared starting a business, on your own?
I would say 'ignorance is bliss'. At the onset, I didn't have much knowledge about doing business, I just leapt into the trading ring, it was a 'dare devil' behavior. But to be honest, I was totally unaware about the risks and dangers involved.

Having said that, I appreciate the support that I got from my colleagues. Without their mentorship I would not have been able to reach where I am today.

In stock broking, you must have learnt by observing 'other people'? Mostly men I suppose?
Yes, that's right.
It took a lot of patience and perseverance.

What was it like, your initial days?
I was initially a layman to the trade, completely ignorant about the tricks of the trade. Even after doing CA, the 'stock market operations' was totally alien to me. The accounting

involved in trading, is totally different. It does not prepare you for trading.

The ride initially towards success was bumpy and rough. The system was totally different from what I had expected. However, as time passed, I worked hard, gained experience and slowly and steadily learnt the intricacies involved.

It was like shop floor training, starting from the lowest level and reaching the highest.

I can proudly say that I was the country's highest taxpayer, at one point of time.

That's must have made you proud? Did you become more confident?
Getting to this point was not at all difficult for me as I had been a high achiever throughout my academic and professional career. In fact, I call myself a 'Daredevil' personality. I believe that with the right amount of effort and determination one can achieve great heights. I am the sort of person who never shirks from taking action and the outcome is automatically good. After all, patience and perseverance pays in the end.

Is this a natural ability you have?
I hail from South Gujarat. Actually South Gujarat women are better known for their guts.

It is said women there are commercial minded?
I won't call them commercial minded but yes, they are professionals. At one point of time, 60% of the women teachers in Bombay Municipal Corporation belonged to the south Gujarat community.

Being the first woman in the stock exchange, did you have the feeling of doing something different?
Actually, I didn't know I was the first woman out there. Only after I went, I came to know that I was the first woman. I think people treated me well, they gave me a lot of respect. Additionally, at that time there were very few chartered accountants who had chosen trading as a career option. So, we got a lot of respect.

Why do you think women are hesitant to become traders?
Unfortunately, the stock market has a negative image. So that's the first problem. Because of this reason, even men are hesitant to take up trading. if you look at the trading ring pictures, even women would not want to go.

Then after you started trading, you were also the first Lady President of the BSE.
Things kept happening one after the other. While being in the trading business, I noticed that there were anomalies in the system, which I decided to 'set right'. Being a person with a 'reformist attitude'. I got into improving things. One thing led to the other and soon I was elected as a prestigious member of the 'Board' of the Exchange with highest vote tally of 99%.

Do you think that there is any difference in the way women trade vs male traders?
No, there is no difference in the way men and women do trading. Now people have understood the worth and value of trading. Earlier they invested. There is a difference in attitude now.

People have realized that stock market is a place where you can invest. In fact, young people are looking at it as a market.

At any point of your life, have you felt like you should have done something else? Nowadays there is a thought process that we should have 2 to 3 options?
Absolutely not. I thoroughly enjoyed what I was doing. I loved it. If I have another life, I will still do the same thing. I have no regrets about anything, whatsoever.

In the Stock Exchange, every broker has unique strategy. What was yours?
Well, we didn't have a rigid strategy that we followed. However, from day one, our objective was, to give the best service and advice to our investors. We have always worked with this principle.

How did you happen to get into improving the stock exchange processes?
Being an analytical person whenever I encounter a problem, I approach it from every possible angle and come to the best possible conclusion. It makes me happy to make things better, improve services. Since I travelled a lot during my BSE Presidency days while doing investor education, I became privy to issues at the exchange, especially those involving service delays. To make amendments, for the better, comes naturally to me.

My peers were always ready to support me. They were ready to teach and I was ready to learn.

There may have been times when your opinions and ideas may have contradicted, especially with your male counterparts, during your 'Presidentship'. How did you handle that?
Ideas conflicted all the time because, I was interested in

bringing about changes in the system, On the other hand, people were used to the old ways; they were resistant to change. Little did they realize the inefficiency of the system.

Initially it was not an easy task. It happened gradually. I think you need to have a positive attitude and need to address each person's concerns individually. Thus, you are able to win their trust.

Secondly, you need to remember that when people criticize, it is your idea they are criticizing and not you. They don't know how to separate the separate the idea from the person. It is not personal, it is professional. If you keep that philosophy in mind, communication breakdowns will never happen.

Do you have anything to say to other women who want to follow in your footsteps?
I think investment is something which everybody needs to take seriously, be it man or woman. Most of the men are good at earning money, but they're not necessarily good at managing money. People make a mess of their finances most of the time because they only do passive investing which is putting all their money in a bank deposit. They don't invest as such. Indian people are extremely averse to investing. You know, the penetration of mutual funds stock markets in India is barely 6 - 7%, as compared to 40 - 50% the world over. So, I think we lack the insight to participate in the markets. There is this huge opportunity here for women to earn an income.

In your view, what is the best professional dress for women?
Saree is my favourite attire. I love to wear saris all the time. Moreover, as I'm on the heavier side, saree is the best bet and it suits me. I think we should wear cool, comfortable clothes

and dress up according to occasion.

I remember having an aunt, who was very particular about clothes. Every time she invited us to her house, she would call up in advance and enquire about our dress. She made sure that we wore decorative and attractive clothes and that we had planned our attire which had to look festive.

What about marriage and career. Do you think both can mix?
Oh yes, very much so. I am a great proponent. I think women should not sit at home; they must work. By work I mean they should have some recreation, either a job, social service or business. Whatever they choose, it is important for them to get out of their house. This way their mind remains healthy as they meet different people. It completely changes the personality and relieves stress. Going out and working is a stress buster especially for women, as they get an opportunity to get away from their household and family problems. If you think you are in pain, by going out and meeting people, you tend to realize how much pain they have. Like, there's a story in which a man complains about not having shoes, until he sees a man without feet.

So, it is important that women go out, meet colleagues and talk about their problems. If you do social work, you meet so many people who are from different section of the society. You get a different perspective, then you realize that you are in a much better situation than most of them.

Nowadays girls want to postpone their marriage, they want to establish themselves in their career, first. Do you think that's a good move?
Even if they marry late, after establishing themselves, then

also the responsibility of the family will be theirs. It is not the timing of the break that matters, it is the length of the break. Important thing is that they should come back to work after a reasonable period. Continuity matters in career. Even if they get married at a late stage, they must continue their careers without a break in their career.

But do you think that for a woman, it is important to get married, to feel fulfilled?
Not really, I think it's better not to marry rather than have a bad marriage. If you find a good partner, then it is worth it. If you don't find a good one, it is better not to marry.

What do you think is the most common mistake women make in their career?
I think first mistake that women make is that they tend to be very emotional in their workplace. You need to be like you are an actor, playing a role. What we read in the Bhagavad Gita all the time. So, what you need to do, if somebody criticizes you, you should take that criticism in a good spirit. You should not take it personally. It should be considered as an opportunity to improve your shortcomings, professionally. If you want to continuously improve, you should weigh criticism as right or wrong. If it is wrong, you may just ignore it; if it is right, you may try to improve on it. But one should not get so much rattled and bogged down by it.

Can you give them some tip on how to take this impersonally?
I would say it is a conditioning of the mindset, it is not that you can achieve it overnight. It took me also many years to master it. It has to become your second nature, that every time somebody

criticizes you then it is not you but your work that is being criticized. I think positively above it. So, I think that is a kind of conditioning of the mind that is required, it is not magic. First you have to believe in that and then you have to continuously motivate yourself, till it becomes second nature to you.

What do you do in your spare time? do you read, what are your hobbies?
Ohh ... I have read 1000s of books literally. I am an avid reader. Of late, I am more into reading and studying spiritual texts, like, the Bhagavad Gita, Hanuman Chalisa, Bhaj Govindam and Bhakvindam. I like listening to discourses, then I make notes and chant them.

I do pranayama every day, I practise grapho therapy (handwriting scinence), I do physical exercises like weights etc.

So, what makes you angry? What moves you?
No, actually, I don't get angry anymore now. It is very difficult to make me angry.

During trading it must be very difficult to keep your emotions in check?
No, it is fun actually. It is a lot of fun.

Now I am aged 60. I have had a career of almost 40 years, now. I have been through all sorts of ups and downs of life. Today, if you ask me, "Do you get angry?" The reply would be in the negative. Maybe if you had asked me 10 years back, the reply would have been positive. But over a period of time, one rises above all these emotions.

Do you have any ambitions now?
Oh, I want to travel the world, that is my current dream. I've been so busy that I have not managed to go anywhere. I've

travelled 47 countries in 40 years but still there are places in the world, waiting to be explored.

Okay. How would you like your peers to remember you?
I would like my peers to remember me as a person who can be relied upon, and above all, a supportive person.

As far as your business philosophy is concerned, is there anything you would like to say?
In fact, I have really not been very successful in communicating this philosophy because a lot of people trade, but I would want people to invest. However, I am still trying to explain to people, about the difference between trading & investing. You can consider this as my business philosophy.

As you progressed, have you scaled up your dreams or have you scaled down your dreams?
No, no, I have realized my dreams to the fullest. I think God has been very kind to me. I have more than what I need. More than, what I'm capable of. I think God has given me more than I deserve.

Why do you think women are not there in Corporate Boards, especially in India?
Women have to raise themselves up. I do not think that someday men are going to come and lift you up. You have to do it yourself. I think women have to help other women. If the mother-in-law encourages the daughter in law, to go and work, it will help. I think it is women who have to help women. If there are other working women in the family, like, your auntie, your sister-in-law, mother-in-law etc. then the kind of approach towards working women would completely

change. The kind of social pressures that you feel, will all go away.

Do you find any major shifts that have happened, since you started your career?
Definitely, attitudes are changing, people are thinking differently, now. People have started accepting women as professionals. The change is happening. With time it will become more evident.

How do you think we can make a difference in these numbers? Do you think in India also, there should be 'mentoring' on a large scale?
It is inevitably going to happen. The government is trying to see to it that there is 'women participation' in boards. There are a lot of independent women directors, now. A few of them approach me for guidance and mentorship, for which I provide full support.

I see some institutions and associations, providing mentoring to aspiring candidates. It's not like, nothing is happening. Lot of organizations are doing things at their level – little bit here, little bit there. The results will take time to become visible. That's all.

In Corporate boards, legislation is there, but how do you think we can bring more women into the management boards?
As I said, it is up to the women. Most of the women drop out of their career, when they have a child, they should be motivated not to do so. You need at least 17 to 18 years of experience in your CV without any break, for rising up to the level of management boards.

"My take on
Deena Mehta

Her upbringing

Deena Mehta grew up in a stable home where she got a lot of attention because she was the only girl. Something about their culture prompted her parents to send her to an English-speaking school, rather than her brother. These positive strokes in the environment translated into her taking risky decisions for the betterment of her family, giving up a good job to start out on an entrepreneurial journey.

Her Pioneership

The profession was incidental, she would have shone anywhere because of her learning attitude that enabled her to master the nitti gritties of trading. Combined with her natural ability to strike a rapport with people who could teach her. She has always used her intelligence in pursuit of improving working for the trading community as a whole and therefore outcomes have been favourable. It is her initiative, ideas, and her style of execution that people aligned with for which she has been rewarded by becoming a pioneer within the same patriarchal culture that we all live and work in.

Gender then becomes incidental.

Leadership

At a very young age she travelled abroad to take part in a global event. That shows the confidence of her parents in her and her comfort with herself, good traits for a leader. After all it can be lonely at the top, with only your vision for company.

As BSE President, the reforms she has carried out, has consolidated her knowledge for which she is respected. Her Integrity and commitment are the hall marks she displayed as a leader.

Women specific

I would not be far from the truth if I were to say that women are absent from some professions not because of their gender but because a woman has not found it worth her while to venture there. Deena has a no-nonsense attitude towards matters of feminine interest – dress comfortably, the lady says. After all people are coming to listen to her views. And also, towards making women successful - depending on the support of other women in the family.

The most important pointer that she gives is stats around penetration of mutual funds in Indian stock markets is barely 6 - 7% compared to 40 - 50% world over. Women wanting to do generate income, having a basic knowledge of Finance. Even Finance students after graduation, can establish themselves as MF advisers and turn entrepreneurs. Institutions that have set up employment training institutes, can use this statistic to train girls as entrepreneurs.

Sucheta Shah
EXECUTIVE DIRECTOR, ATLAS INTEGRATED FINANCE LTD

HOW A MATHS and Chemistry topper (in school) and a dance enthusiast reaches the echelons of Corporate Boards, including one of the most respected companies in India, is a story worth telling young girls choosing their subjects in Class 9. Sucheta's has been a story which shows how a woman balances her family and career. I have been exposed to her leadership style as co-member in FICCI FLO, a very unobtrusive, humble lady. Today when having company names in your aanchal is a status symbol, she prefers to be known for her work. She is one of the more sought-after names on the Independent Directors roster.

Sucheta's career story stands out as a role model of how with the right subject matter expertise, experience and networking skills, India can be among the topmost companies in the World Economic Forum rankings for Women in Corporate Boards.

Here is a list of her corporate experiences:
- ❖ Atlas Integrated Finance Ltd, April 1994 - Present (28 years 7 months) Mumbai as Executive Director, a Wealth Management. SEBI Registered Portfolio Manager. Mumbai, India.

- ❖ Independent Director on Corporate Boards - Tata Housing Development Co. Ltd., Infopark Properties Ltd., The Indian Hume Pipe Co. Ltd., Jayant Agro Oils Ltd., Ishedu Agrochem Pvt Ltd. and Landmark Cars ltd.
- ❖ Founder https://msmedirect.com
- ❖ FICCI MSME Sector, April 2018 - November 2020 (2 years 8 months), Chair - Maharashtra State Committee
- ❖ Grameen Initiative for Women, October 2007 - March 2019 (11 years 6 months), Promoter Director - A Section 8 Company working towards upliftment of Economically backward Women.
- ❖ FICCI FLO April 2011 - April 2012 (1 year) FICCI FLO Mumbai – Chairperson followed by a 3-year stint as National Head - SWAYAM (A Support Cell for Women Entrepreneurs)
- ❖ Chaturvedi & Shah - Management Team- Merchant Banking April 1991 - March 1995 (4 yrs.)

Her academic choices, which she discusses in some detail in the interview, include the following:
1. MMS Finance - SP Jain Institute of Management & Research. (SPJIMR)
2. B Com - Sydenham College of Commerce and Economics

Sun, 12/12 11:51AM • 58:57

Let us hear about your upbringing. Were you brought up in a joint family or a nuclear family? Did your father serve the government, was he a professional in a private firm or did he run a family business?

I come from a business family; My father was an MS from Purdue University, with a degree in pharma. He was a gold medallist. Our family business was in pharmaceutical trading. We are Gujarati Jains.

As far as my memory goes, the first 10 years of my childhood were spent in a joint family. There were almost 14 to 15 members sharing the same house. This included my father's brothers, who were getting married. As our family grew bigger and bigger, space started becoming a constraint. So, we shifted to another house and became a nuclear family.

One advantage of a joint family is that children are looked after and brought up jointly by uncles and aunts. I have a younger brother, who is three years younger to me. My mom is a proud graduate and a high achiever. Till the time we were in the joint family, she was always busy with household chores. But when we became nuclear. she could pursue her interests, go swimming, she liked painting, she was a very good artist. At the same time, she made sure that we were well taken care of. She chose to remain primarily a housewife, so that she could focus on our upbringing.

My father wanted me to become an IAS or an IFS officer. MBA was not given importance at that time. Out of all the people, he inspired me the most. He taught me Science because he was very good at Maths and Science. I don't remember taking any tuitions, like most children do these days. I always managed on my own. This tradition was upheld by my children as well.

What was the environment like at home? Was it very traditional? Were there any differences as far as bringing up son versus daughter is concerned?
No, it wasn't traditional at all. My father had studied abroad so he had a broader perspective to life. In spite of that, we were not given total freedom but yes there was motivation to do well in life. There were certain things that we were not allowed, like late nights. In terms of treatment, both me and my brother were treated equally as we were given the freedom to make our own career choices. There was no limiting factor.

The only thing they wanted was that we should study sincerely so as to be successful in life. I made the most of this opportunity and always came out with flying colours. I became the university ranker. In fact, I have been a high achiever throughout my academic career. The credit goes to my parents who forever motivated us to do well in life.

What was school life like? Who were you in school - The teacher's pet, the class bully, the mouse or the back bencher? How did that shape you?
Most of the teachers liked me and appreciated my enthusiasm towards academics. My handwriting was also impressive. Even though I lacked in sports, I can be labelled as an all-rounder, as I was a Prefect in school. I was always among the first three / four rankers. My mom was keen that I take up 'performing arts' as an activity choice in school. I have given

my 'Arangetram' in dance. In fact, at one stage of my life, I thought of pursuing a career in dance.

I was also good at public speaking. My participation in inter-school, dramatics, gave me opportunities to meet people from other schools, which widened my horizons. I topped in Maths and Chemistry in my school.

At this point I was in two minds, whether to opt for dance or pursue academics for professional career. I was good at both. My Maths teacher advised me to pursue dance as a 'hobby' and to take up a professional career, as it had better prospects. I found the suggestion quite reasonable. In the field of dance, after certain age, somebody younger or somebody better comes along. But the IQ and reasoning of the brain never diminishes. I took that advice and continued both side by side.

From which college of Bombay University did you study?
I graduated from Sydenham College of Commerce & Economics, Mumbai (B. Com), after which I did my post-graduation in Finance from S P Jain institute of Management & Research (MBA).

When did you start thinking about MBA as a career route? Is there any particular incident which was the turning point – which influenced your career choice?
Both CA and MBA were equally good options at that time. But the decision happened gradually. After my 12th std., I decided to take admission in a prestigious college - Sydenham. It was well known for diverse activities and societies that I couldn't resist the temptation of exploring it.

I did not take up science even though I scored good marks and had a knack for it. The reason being I wanted to explore new avenues, apart from the traditional science fields.

I was young, I had dreams, so I took up commerce. I wanted the finer things in life and I thought commerce would help me do that.

I joined the Performing Arts Society, Public Speaking, debating society and eventually was on their managing committee in Sydenham College.

After my 12th std., again, I had a choice to start my CA internship. Mostly people did that along with their FY BCom. But I did not want that, I wanted to take up that option after my graduation.

At that point of time MBA had just come into play. I decided to take this option as it would widen the scope of opportunities. I could start my own business, or take up a job somewhere, I did not want to be stuck to tax and accounting only. In fact, even though I had scored 98% in accounts, I still wanted another option, so I decided to take admission in SPJIMR.

What was that extra edge which your college gave as far as your career is concerned?
It is the extra mile you go, that will make you better than the rest. I was lucky to get tuition from the best of professors, for the main accounts paper, so that helped.

What Sydenham really did was bring out the leadership qualities in my good self. I organized many events, one of which is still 'the most talked about'. I had organized an exhibition of instruments used in performing arts - like the wind instrument, the pipe, the strings and percussion. The special feature of that event was the guest list which included the very famous Shiv Kumar Sharma and Zakir Husain,

Organizing these events and inviting such legendary artists, made all the difference.

We invited JRD Tata and Amin Sayani. Listening to their motivational talks was a huge game changer. I think Sydenham was THE place which helped us to stand out.

After MBA, where did you acquire your professional education and training?

I took up' finance' as a specialization, which helped me bag a position in the Merchant banking division of CanBank financial services for one year.

Then I got married. It was an arranged marriage. My husband is an electrical engineer from Veermata Jijabhai Technical Institute, Mumbai with an administrative Management diploma from Jamanalal Bajaj Institute of management studies. My mother-in-law is also a BA from Xavier's college, Mumbai. My parents were pretty sure that since my future husband is educated, and comes from a good family, things would be fine.

In fact, after a few months my mother-in-law supported me and I took up a job with flexi hours. No doubt it meant more hard work, it was a step forward. I took it very positively. It was a financial services firm. Initially it was not easy as I had to manage the household chores and the job pressure. During those days, families were more conservative, my husband was also settling down in his business, it was becoming difficult for me to balance home and work, so I quit my job. Then I had kids.

After a few years, I got a very good break with a CA firm - Chaturvedi and Shah. There too I had flexi hours. I grabbed this opportunity as I had got the much-needed break for my career. They are a very big audit firm, with a huge Merchant banking division, better known as 'investment banking'. They gave me full flexible working hours which helped me manage my work and children. I would go home in the afternoon and return to work in the evening. The best thing was, it was close to my house. This saved me travel time. But then if I had a client calling me up at eight in the night, I had to attend the call.

That five-year period flew by so quickly, I found myself on top of the world as both my personal and professional life was giving me much satisfaction. I had the best of clients. I was lucky enough to gain experience in both fields - investment banking and project finance.

What was your thinking process when you chose 'Finance' as your career? Did it have any influence on your personality or your career opportunities?

That was the time, when educating women was being given some importance. Travelling to places, was still unthinkable for women. That being said, I still opted for a career in this field. I took up finance as I was good with numbers, and I would have to do less travelling.

In fact, there was a phase during 1994 - 95, when my kids were five, I felt my children needed more of my time than I was giving them, So I switched to two, three hours of research work only. This continued for three to four years. During this time, we (my husband & I) took up the stock exchange membership. Then I got into working full-time.

Then of course, in 2002 I joined FICCI Ladies Organization. As my kids grew up, I devoted more time to social projects. The support that I got from my family helped me grow professionally.

Can you talk about your career growth? What made a difference?

I give full credit to my mother-in-law for supporting me, due to which, I could devote my full attention to our business. That is how it grew. Moreover, the client's demands and needs keep you on your toes and helps you to bloom professionally.

Another important factor which helps in the growth process is networking. I am a member of FICCI FLO (Federation of Indian Chambers of Commerce and Industry) and my husband is a Rotary member. How I got my first directorship is an e.g. of how well you connect with other organizations. Just doing your work is not enough. You have to go the extra mile. You have to connect with others. You never know when a connection may click and help you bag your dream position. What works where, what helps when, you never know. It just flows.

If your career is important, your business is important, meeting people and networking is a prerequisite if you want to be successful. Every drop makes an ocean. The opportunity may not come immediately, it may take weeks, months or even years for the right opportunity to come along. Patience makes a man wiser and richer. At the end of the day your capability shines in the form of success. Media waits on you to pen down your interviews everywhere.

One thing I have learnt from my experience is that you just don't have to stick to doing your business, but give time to other things as well. I am happy, in the long run it worked out well for me. It may be different for others though.

What would be your advice to young women about to commence their career?
There is this one incident which I must share with everybody. I had an aunt, a designer. She had given up her career and then restarted after her kids had finished 10th Std. She advised me not to give up my career totally after marriage. "Even if it is

two to three hours a day, make sure you are working" she had said. So that you are in touch with your field; because when you get out of touch, it is very difficult for most women to make a comeback. So, I made sure till my ninth month of pregnancy, I kept working.

Strong will power and determination helps you to move forward. If you are firm and confident then nobody can take you for granted, or mislead you. You just have to be firm and confident. Initially my mother-in-law was not in favor of my working full time. But when she realized, we're both doing well and growing, that made her change her mind. in fact, she started taking care of the house, in my absence. I trusted her and never had any complaints.

Everything happened gradually. Rome was not built in a day. If we move forward with patience, we can win over a million hearts. When I was young, I had been impatient and made a lot of mistakes, but I learned that if you have patience, people around you are ready to accommodate and adjust. When they see you excelling in your field, they start trusting you.

That being said, giving due importance to family and career, both, is important. Both have to be balanced.

One positive lesson that I learnt in life is not to get upset if somebody says' No'. There have been times when people have point blank refused to do a certain thing. But you should take it in your stride because if one door closes, a bigger one opens. Let me quote a real-life example to support this statement. I had been in the FLO Mumbai committee for quite some time, and then in the National Committee, again for a longer time than expected. So I decided to take a step back. As a result, that door closed. But I got a better opportunity and I got the FICCI Maharashtra MSME Chair. We should never be disheartened with failures, because it is only with perseverance one reaches the top.

Marriage & Career or Marriage or Career? Do you think one has to sacrifice their career for marriage? Does marriage have anything to do with feeling fulfilled in life?

What I feel is that at some point of time, marriage is more important, and at others, marriage is not important. You have to keep choosing every moment, every hour and every day, it depends. During the growing up years of my kids, I never stopped working.

Our family life too faced its share of challenges, but we learnt to navigate them. When I was busy at work, my husband held the fort at home. And when family needs were there, I held the fort. My brother-in-law, who was seven years younger to my husband, met with an accident and expired. He was only 24 / 25 years of age. My mother-in-law was devastated. I made this decision to be with her for almost eight to 10 months. I chose to work from home. There were no laptops at that time, just desk tops which were bulky and cumbersome to use. I made myself available for the family in their time of adversity. These things brought me closer to my family and I can proudly say that at this stage of my life family came first for me. So, one weighs over the other at different stages of your life.

Every day in your career, you have to make important choices, be it good or bad, the key is to keep going. Just try your best and if at any point of time, you have to make a choice, choose what's more important. My goal has been to do well in life overall, in terms of career and family, even if it meant sacrificing a few things here and there. I wouldn't call them sacrifices, but certain things do get delayed. Fame and success will come to you, if you put your heart and soul in it. It is rightly said - Hard work is the key to success. If you really want something, keep trying!

Be persistent in achieving your ambition. If you want to become a CEO at 35, keep working for it. It's your goal. Be sure to move forward with every bit of dedication and sincerity that you have. But if you want leverage, then it's better to be happy with the smaller things in life.

Careers and Family go hand in hand. Both are important.

What about temptations like other lucrative offers abroad instead of following the well beaten path? What did you struggle with, in the initial years?
We started off from ground zero; to get that network itself was really difficult. We were surrounded by big firms, but still we kept on. We were in the stock market, econo-derivative, currency market, and a depository licenses, to name a few. We kept adding one every year because we couldn't do it all at one go. We had no money to start with, so we had to first make money then take the license. Consequently, the growth was slow and steady till 2010-11. We were happy with it.

Then we both were very busy in our social networking – my husband in Rotary and myself with FICCI FLO. Suddenly we had too many social projects in hand. After that, I became the chairperson in 2011-12. Business was growing but since we could not give a hundred per cent, it suffered. Things were fine, but not growing. We also realized that none of our children wanted to join us. For this reason, we decided to keep it small and not to aspire for more than what we had already achieved. Our satisfaction level was optimum as it is not easy to reach here from scratch. We have our niche class, our HNI and a good set of clients. So far so good. I feel that maybe if we would have grown much more, then I would have not been able to do the other finer things in life, like networking which was important to me as well as to my husband. We decided to grow in a few divisions only.

In your opinion, what is the ideal professional dress for women?
My work clothes have always been trousers. It doesn't matter. But when I go as an independent director, I wear a saree. Saree, I feel, earns you respect when you are amongst senior people and in important meetings also saree fits in very well. Broadly speaking, I have no personal preferences.

From whom did you imbibe your early leadership lessons?
I did my MBA, internship at ICICI Bank Merchant banking division, under Renuka Ramnath. That is where my best learning lessons were learnt. She was my first boss. So actually I was lucky to get such experienced and skilful people as my bosses, early in life.

I was fortunate enough to have worked in companies which had very good clientele.

When I started on my own, we were into NSE / BSE trading, stock trading and mutual funds. Thereafter there was a switch over in my field of work. I got more into research and portfolios. We were able to get good clients, as the stock market was booming,

Did India's patriarchal culture ever become difficult to manage? Would you like to share your secret in handling it?
On the contrary, my experience with the managements have been fantastic. For any company management to grow, it is

very essential to lend an ear to everybody's points of view, other than your own. Then make sure that certain points made are recorded and minuted. Final decision is the management's prerogative.

For an independent director, most important point to look for, in a company, is the management. Everything else is secondary. If the management is strong and positive, we have a very fine balance between the investors and management. I make sure to put in my point of view. What decision they make is not in your hands. But you make sure that it is minuted.

As for our own clients, it's all about delivering. Client expectations always kept us on our toes. Then there was no question of facing any kind of bias.

Tell me something about what motivates you, what do you like doing in your spare time?
I like reading and dancing. Performing arts is my passion. Sometimes I go to NCPA to see performances. My husband accompanies me sometimes or I go on my own.

Regarding lack of women directors, where do you think the remedy lies? I would like to hear your take on it.
Having women reservation is a debatable issue. You see most of the businesses in India are family owned. Among them, skilled professionals are very few. So what is happening is that the trust factor for independent directors is better. After all, businesses want to do well. As Independent Directors, management wants to make sure the person has a bit of experience. However here everything works on trust. Nobody wants to employ a completely unknown person as director. Even a little bit of acquaintance with the person builds trust in the person.

Professionalism is not that prevalent in businesses. That needs to grow. Now I feel women are recognized more for what they bring to the table. People trust them to take more responsibilities than before. Circumstances are becoming favourable for women. Disparity between women-men in my view, is decreasing by the day. Knowledge and skill have more value, rather than status-quo. Things are changing for the better.

Cooperation and flexibility are a must, to be in the flow. There was a time when I was managing so much-kids, family, home, that too without any help. Without losing heart and my husband's support I carried on. We could spend quality time with our two children who are now adults and excelling in their own career.

Our commitment brought us client trust, which helped us. It's all worth it, in the end.

Where, what, when it will work, you don't know …just keep doing!

" My take on Sucheta Shah

Leadership

Reading these 2 interviews from finance industry, Deena and Sucheta, it seems like women have found the niche where they can make an impact. Their career story moves on different paths because both had different life situations, yet they rode the balance of talent and life very well. The similarity is not that both are MBAs, but that both see that for women to dominate board rooms, it is a matter of time and merit garnered from experience. Both have earned respect for their knowledge and contribution, yet they have their unique styles. Deena is a straight shooter, while Sucheta wears her power very humbly.

What is meaningful for me that both women have nowhere used the word objective or targets, even though they are very successful women. The words that dominate are behavioural, on "Being".

Her well-rounded personality is reflected in the equal importance she gives to work, family and enjoying the finer things in life.

Her upbringing
The seeds of the future lie in the past as seen in Sucheta's upbringing. The focus given to academics at home laid the foundation of her expertise, but it is in her extra-curricular activities that she found the source of her leadership. Her initiative and genuine interest in music brought industry leaders and artists big wigs to share knowledge which has laid the foundation of her networking ability.

She is the perfect example for me to point out how and why extra-curricular activities determine your altitude.

Women specific
Just like Sucheta took her Professor Aunt's advice to heart, "whatever you do Sucheta, even if it is two to three hours a day, make sure you are working. …… ……….. to bring that back" I find many gems which women aspiring to be Directors on Boards can take to heart. Both interviews reflect how important it is for the extended family to support women's endeavours.

You must be firm and confident before you can win over others.

Vijayalaxmi Chabbra
EX DIRECTOR GENERAL, DOORDARSHAN

WHEN YOU TALK to Vijayalaxmi, you get the feeling of resolute strength. That's how a girl from a small steel township comes to Delhi and reaches the position of Director General of Doordarshan, the world's biggest Public Service Broadcaster. I don't know what to talk about more – her domain expertise in content creation & social communication or her innate capability to connect with people, purely on her communication ability. All India Radio must have been glad to have her. She has made innumerable award-winning radio documentaries on social issues. Her career is a reflection of post-Independence India, where men and women had the fervour to build strong institutions in India and generally contribute to nation building. That was the time when jobs were not about me or my job satisfaction, but about playing a role in something larger than yourself.

It started with her parent's dream – to make their children successful professionals. Nowadays it is fashionable to blame parents for having those dreams. But today if India stands strong on the world stage, then these parents are responsible.

Over a 35-year career, Vijayaji worked in key positions in All India Radio and Doordarshan. She has many nuggets to give about the working culture of All India Radio & Doordarshan and for women in general.

Here are a few highlights from her career:

- Joined All India Radio in 1980 as a programme officer.
- Posted in Doordarshan in the year 2000.
- Awarded Commonwealth Fellowship in the year 1995 to study privatisation of Radio & Community Radio in UK.
- In mid-career shifted to a marketing & sales role as Director (Marketing & Sales) for Prasar Bharati, where she was hugely successful in marketing Public Service content which is generally considered 'less marketable'.
- Wide exposure to the dynamics of the growing media market in India. She is widely respected in the media circles as an expert on social content marketing and sports (BCCI cricket series in India for 4 years while DD & AIR had the broadcast & telecast rights).
- Her dabbling in social content media continued even post-retirement in 2015. Read the interesting story of how she became a media celebrity. What had started as a hobby to keep herself relevant & still be part of "New Media," she started writing about Indian handlooms which she was passionate about. Her Instagram https://www.instagram.com/vijayalaxmichhabra/ today boasts of more than 53,000/ followers, making her a leading influencer.
- Her page has become almost like a book on various weaves from different Indian States peppered with inspirational stories from her broadcasting career. Along with handloom she writes about women empowerment, family values and her travel stories.

Her career is an outcome of the commitment to excellence

which was inculcated in school:
1. Appeared in the merit list of Madhya Pradesh Higher Secondary School Certificate Exam.
2. BA honours in Political Science from Indraprastha College for Women, Delhi University.
3. MA in Political Science from Indraprastha College for Women, Delhi University.
4. Journalism from Bhartiya Vidya Bhavan.
5. Stood first in UPSC exam to join Indian Broadcasting Service.

Hope this is enough to whet your appetite?

Wed, 4/27 4:15PM • 58:17

What was your upbringing like? Was yours a joint family or a nuclear family?
I was brought up in a completely Odia home. I have observed that when people stay in their own state, they adopt various customs and food habits of other states. But when they move out of their state, they get frozen in time. My upbringing is from the latter category. We lived in Bhilai, Chhattisgarh. My parents kept Odia culture alive in our day-to-day life. They spoke to us in Odia, though we brothers and sisters, spoke to each other in Hindi. Hindi was the spoken language of Chhattisgarh. All Odia festivals were celebrated, my mother prepared Odiya delicacies at home. So, it was completely an Odia home. I'm glad they kept it like that because at least we were exposed to the beautiful & rich culture of Odisha. When you live outside your home state you tend to forget your own traditions. You can roam the whole world, you can appreciate

other cultures, learn whatever you want, but I think it's good to be close to your roots.

My parent's family was primarily a nuclear family; but they did bring up my Chacha and my Bua. My father was the eldest son, so my parents were expected to take care of the younger siblings. Our family did end up being like a joint family. My grandparents too often visited us in Bhilai. They were alive until I was in class nine. We always had guests visiting us. My uncle would drop in every weekend as he was in a city close by, in Brajraj Nagar.

As I said, ours was a nuclear family but always full of people because my parents were very hospitable. Like any other typical family, guests were always welcome, lot of food was being cooked. My mother's kitchen remained open until late night.

After school I joined Delhi University for higher studies. Got married in Delhi. I lived in a real proper Punjabi joint family. Living in that family was the most beautiful experience. My husband's maternal Grandmother, his parents & his uncle, aunt with their children we all lived together under one roof though on different floors. My in-laws were extremely nice, very liberal people. After living almost for 7 years with them I finally moved to Mumbai & set up my own home. Even after moving, I was very closely connected with them. They often visited us and helped looking after our children because I was working. I love having people around me. My younger son, daughter-in-law and my grandson continue to live with us.

I understand your father worked in Bhilai steel plant. What was it like being brought up in a township which was the nation's pride?
I love reminiscing about my beautiful childhood.

I was always very proud of being born in free India. Our parents would often talk about the freedom struggle because it was still fresh in their minds. My mother's family was quite involved in the freedom movement. My mother's maternal grandfather became the first Chief Minister of Odisha soon after India attained freedom. They were all Gandhians and followers of Indian National Congress. Everything was so idealistic. They were such proud people. We were at an age when country was young & everything was being built. My father was in Bhilai, few of his friends were in Hirakud or Bhakra. Some were also in Indian railways.

Whenever they met their conversations centred around how the nation was being built. We children grew up listening to the stories of Nation building.

Was the environment very strict? Were there any differences as far as bringing up son versus daughter is concerned?
We did live in a disciplined environment. There was no discrimination between my brother & me. In fact, I was the eldest so got access to all their resources before my younger siblings could get it. I also feel in eastern India a girl child is more respected as compared to northern India. Sometimes I felt privileged because being the eldest, my family had pinned all hopes on me. So, I got everything first compared to my siblings. My mother was very keen that I must study and do well. It is not easy being the first child of ambitious parents. I was always under great pressure to perform well until I got my first job. Mine is a success story of a small-town girl.

I was inspired to aspire big in a small town though the modernity of that small town facilitated me.

What about education? Were you the hard-working child or the class prefect or the backbencher? And how did that shape you?

Our education in Bhilai was absolutely brilliant because of our teachers. From the very beginning, we were all brought up with a sense of excellence. We had to perform well. Every parent in Bhilai was working hard on their children wanting them to be high achievers. This had an impact on all four of us. We ended up doing quite well in life professionally. I suppose it was the environment of living in a modern and progressive township where everyone was talking about nation building.

Our parents believed that our generation was to carry on with the work their generation had initiated in terms of ideology, infrastructure building for a new nation & in terms of laying the foundation of a progressive economy.

I give credit to my mom for she was the driving force behind our solid education and our financial independence. My mother was very clear that all of us were not studying for the heck of studying. we had to work, be financially independent. I want to see you at the top of your career, she said. She was not highly educated, so to fulfil her dreams she made sure that her daughter studied. I think in Odisha a lot of people were encouraging their daughters to work. My cousins, all were doing something or the other; if nothing, then teaching in schools, colleges, becoming bureaucrats or doctors or engineers, nobody was sitting idle at home.

I went to Delhi University for my higher education. Initially, it was really tough. But I think small town people have that killer instinct to adapt & do well. For most of us it was a big thing, being a woman to get into a big job, reach the top. Most of the women did well. Women were made equipped to multitask.

Education was a very important thing. Today education has come to represent a ticket to go abroad. There was a different kind of pride associated with education. Literacy rate was very low, so education was considered important for emancipation. People thought that their children will become liberal in their thinking because of education. Today it is a means to make money.

That was one very big subtle difference. That's what shaped us.

My father came from a village and by the time he was going to school, zamindari system had been abolished. They were like anyone else struggling for new beginnings in a new nation. My grandpa had to move away from the village to look for a job, he was working with the King of Parikud. My grandmother was bringing up three children. I remember my grandmother telling me that she decided to make her son the first engineer of their village against all odds. My father was a brilliant student all through his school & college. He topped school board and is a gold medallist from Kakinada Engineering college. We were constantly reminded about the hardship, how he studied, how he did well, my mother valued his education so much. She valued it because they were able to afford a good life. She had seen luxuries of a zamindari household and then the hardships after zamindari were abolished. Her observation was that people who took advantage and studied were wiser and had re-established themselves.

In your view, what is that which makes a difference? In whether women give up or not on their careers?
I think it's up to the parents how to shape up their daughters. Education is just not a degree or a decoration. I was clear from the beginning that even though the person I marry is doing

well I would continue to work, never give up my job. My husband was doing brilliantly well in corporate sector. I was in a government job & was not earning the kind of money he was earning yet there was no question of giving up my job.

Today, there are more options, you can work from home. In our time, there was no concept of working from home, you had to go out to work, leave your children behind, which was the toughest part. But we did find ways. It was easier to find help those days. People are more aware today of the downside of leaving children behind with house helps. We had no option; I trusted my helps and support staff. I was forever running around but I managed, I did manage to supervise my children's education, I would plan my leave for their exams and when they fell sick. It was tough but my generation managed.

By the time you are at the middle management level your children are grown up then you can concentrate on your career.

However, you can't generalize. I would not advise you to be judgmental about why women choose to stay at home. Probably being financially independent is not a matter of life & death for them (on an ideological level).

You were responsible for selling the commercial rights of live cricket telecast for Doordarshan. How did that come about?

#Mycricketstories-
Let me give you the context first. DD and cricket had a symbiotic relationship until satellite channels came into the picture. AIR was first to bring in live cricket commentary not only to every Indian home but also thanks to the transistor, it was relayed to the fields, to roadside Dhabas, to moving vehicles. Doordarshan went many steps ahead by bringing

the excitement of live cricket telecasts to millions of antenna homes. As you know in this country, cricket is not only a game, it is a religion. It became the biggest entertainer and revenue garner for the broadcaster as well as for organizers like ICC & BCCI which made huge profits through Broadcast/Telecast Rights Fee.

To be able to show cricket live to millions of Indians, DD had to buy the telecast rights, which could run into crores. To recover this cost DD had to sell commercial time in between the games. My team's job was to raise commercial revenue from live cricket telecast & other programmes on DD. This was a new division set up by me. DD had the biggest property, BCCI cricket. Between 2000 to 2006 my team & I had an important role to play in bringing cricket to millions of homes.

The special story behind how I was instrumental in getting the cricket telecasting rights for Doordarshan happened in 2004. We were anxiously waiting for the Broadcast Rights of much awaited India & Pakistan series, to be played in Pakistan, after 10 years. To our utter surprise a brand-new private satellite sports channel bought the complete & exclusive rights for this particular series. In 2004 the satellite viewing was only 40% as against DD National's terrestrial viewing of 60%. In addition, DD also had a satellite sports channel DD Sports covering 40% of satellite viewing. With these 2 channels DD reached every TV home.

This sports channel didn't have a terrestrial transmission, which would have deprived millions of terrestrial viewers (antenna homes) of this historical cricket series. A handsome sum was offered to the private channel by DD management to buy terrestrial rights, which was turned down. This had never happened in the sports broadcast history of India, as cricket, for us DD walas was more of an emotion.

Public litigation followed. The match was on a Saturday. On Friday evening Supreme Court pronounced that DD National will carry the dirty feed of the private channel to facilitate terrestrial viewers (a dirty feed means relaying another channel with their logo and their ads). Though in public interest it was most insulting for the National Broadcaster, senior management was helpless since it was Supreme Court's Order.

In the evening as I was on my way home when my mobile rang. CEO Prasar Bharati was on line. He wanted to know if we have the technology to superimpose our ads on their feed. I understood what he was hinting at. Are you giving me permission to go ahead and sell it without having the rights??? I exclaimed!!

I could already feel the excitement. I asked my driver to take a U turn and drive me back to my office in Worli. CEO had already consulted Solicitor General. First match was scheduled next morning on a Saturday followed by match on Sunday. Courts would be closed. The rival channel wouldn't be able to take a stay. CEO said, just go ahead. tonight, is yours, do what you want. Remember you have just few hours ... Don't call me again. We will face the consequences on Monday.

All my key officers were called back. It was the most adventurous night of my life. While the whole world slept, we were waging a war against the injustice done towards 170 million TV viewers living in antenna homes.

We woke up the entire advertising industry. Surprisingly no one questioned rather they were extremely supportive. That's the kind of blind faith they had on DD. In next two hours we sold our complete inventory of 5000 seconds at a premium rate. By 6 AM we were ready with our commercial cue sheet. The work at Mumbai end was complete. Head of DD Delhi, a dear friend & colleague extended all support by deputing his best officers on commercial execution panel.

Sharp at 9 am DD rolled its live telecast with its own logo, with its own ads. All premium clients were on board. At 8.30 am, we decided not to carry the dirty feed. Instead, we carried the clean feed provided to us for highlights. Our officers executing the cricket telecast in DD control room worked like warriors that day.

On Monday as expected the matter was in legal arena. What happened next is in public domain.

After this controversial cricket telecast, Govt brought in new legislation which made it mandatory for exclusive right holders (satellite channels) of sports events to compulsorily part with the terrestrial rights to DD-National (which is the only terrestrial channel) with the provision of revenue share.

I still get goose bumps thinking about that night. My management, my colleagues, my counterpart in Delhi, we all took the dangerous risk. We did all this only because it was cricket. All of us actually celebrated our work that night in anticipation of seeing this historical match on DD National - "Desh ka Apna Channel".

India won that series in Pakistan and next year when Pakistan visited India for the return series, BCCI handed over the exclusive rights to DD.

Sports didn't come to me easy. It wasn't my forte but selling was my forte. My husband who played cricket in DU taught me nuances of the game. I had to earn the confidence and respect of my male colleagues who were taking orders from me & quietly waiting and watching to see how much of cricket I knew. However, being a woman never came in my way as I diligently learnt ball by ball cricket.

All India Radio and Doordarshan, being bureaucratic organization, did you ever find any male bias there?

No, no, I was very fortunate. There was no discrimination Neither in All India Radio (AIR) nor in Doordarshan (DD) because I was a woman. There were more men in AIR and DD as compared to women yet the women employees were equally important. Voices of women presenters were loved & appreciated on air. AIR is much older than DD, so there were a lot of women working, anybody who had a creative urge, got into AIR. There were renowned female voices - Indu Wahi, Pamela Singh, Lotika Ratnam who read Prime Time news, Female announcers of Vividh Bharati were equally popular.

Key to success was working hard. It was an organisation where women were appreciated for their special creative skills.

I had cleared a competitive exam conducted by UPSC called Indian Broadcasting Service. So, there was no question of anybody discriminating against someone like me. In fact, I had topped my batch of Programme Executives when I joined Indian Broadcasting Service. There was a fair amount of competition. Later by the time DD happened, because it was a visual medium, many women came into the profession. They looked much better on screen. There were more women news readers than men, both in Hindi and English.

Nobody took women casually because there were brilliant women officers and presenters.

It was primarily a skill-based organisation where your gender really did not matter; what mattered was quality of your work and how much your listeners and viewers loved you. So, I think I was fortunate to be working in an organization where I never felt I was discriminated against only because I was a woman.

Also, a lot is up to you. I was brought up probably differently, many people often have asked me this question. I never felt discriminated against because my parents treated my brother and me equally. I was given a fair chance. I even topped my UPSC selection list. As far as postings were concerned also it was all merit driven.

Where and how did you acquire your professional mastery and training? What influence did your peer group have on your leadership style?

I have been influenced by my senior broadcasters. It's difficult to name each one of them. There was a time when all of us wanted to speak like them. Ashok Bajpai, Devki Nandan Pandey, Lotika Ratnam. They were the first voices that we heard. We learnt everything from them. Many of my Station Directors too influenced the way I thought and worked. I cannot name just one person, so many people have influenced me. I entered AIR as a very raw talent, someone very well educated not knowing broadcasting at all. Whatever I am today is the result of what I learnt from my seniors. The way I think, the way I see things, the way I managed my staff and station and later the whole organisation was all learnt from my seniors.

We were very particular about small details. We were trained to be punctual. We were told we were the time keepers of the Nation.

We said "it is 9 am and now listen to the news". People would match their clocks with our announcements. So how can we be even few seconds late. We were not allowed to enter the meeting if we're late.

These are the small things we were taught. It was like a finishing school. It was not merely an organization. I learnt how to drape my sarees smartly from my women bosses. I learnt to speak immaculately from my seniors. There was so much emphasis in AIR to speak well. Somebody who couldn't speak well, was not considered good enough. So that's the first thing we learnt that we have to speak well, to have mastery over one language at least. Hindi was my language of broadcast. I remember one of those stories that I narrated. I have many stories, "Meri baat aap ke naam". Do listen to them whenever you get a chance. It is a video recording where I have narrated some of the world's famous stories, in Hindi. They are available in the guide on my Instagram handle.

I always wanted to be remembered as an efficient administrator. Because back in the day, it was all about how I ran my organization, how I managed, took care of our organization.

What do you think is the ideal professional dress for women?
Well, we wore saris. Saree was the most sought-after professional dress in a respectable position, the senior officers couldn't think of wearing anything else. In our office salwar kameez was worn once in a while only by the junior staff who were also very young or straight from college. They too took to sarees after few years. I went everywhere in my sarees, all international conferences, all important meetings saree was the dress code. All senior women bureaucrats draped sarees. Our woman Prime Minister at that point of time was quite an inspiration. I don't know when and how Saree disappeared from the life of professional women. People now have to make an effort.

It's only a notion that saree is difficult to manage, it's not. I would say Saree is power dressing. No other dress exudes so much power, not even a business suit.

I draped simple and affordable sarees as my daily attire. I take great care of them. I have preserved them for so many years. They look special because no one weaves those designs anymore. My sarees were like anybody else's except that I wore only handloom, I don't wear synthetic and other fabrics. Post retirement it translated into a second career for me when I started writing about them on social media.

I understand you have created quite an active following on your Instagram handle?
It all happened quite by chance actually. By the time I retired, Facebook had started, I had opened an account, and by chance I came across one of these saree groups, somebody must have added me. I started seeing it in my feeds. Nobody was really writing anything. They were just posting their pictures. I started writing stories about sarees. Lots of people appreciated it. It went on for one to two years. Then my children said that if you want to write then you might as well join Instagram. My daughter opened a page for me on Instagram, I started curating my page. By that time, I had a fairly good idea as to what I wanted my page to look like. It had to have content; it was not about posting my pictures. I started writing when I was 61. Nobody's coming to my page to look at my face or my pictures. I was very clear that it had to be content driven. I started writing about handloom sarees. I also started writing about various interesting incidents of my career.

There are one or two areas that I focus on. One is the weave, the other is my career. As a woman, how I took up challenges, so that young girls can be inspired, that they need to work and be financially independent. I talk a lot about women empowerment through financial independence. I often write about incidents from my own life to make it sound real and achievable. I was like anybody else, running around trying to multitask. I wasn't always Director General. I started as a program officer just like any other person. So, it's possible.

Now Instagram is really very dear thing in my life. I have met so many young people, I have made friendships, I think I'm able to make a very small difference. Nevertheless, lots of people write to me that they started to wear saree after reading my posts. They write to me ma'am, I have my IAS interview, what kind of saree should I wear? It makes me feel good. Every day I write about 2200 words. This is a new career for me, being on social media, where I mostly interact with younger people. It was a challenge carving a place for myself among the young crowd. Let me be very honest, I feel very good about it. Standing out in the crowd of beautiful young talented girls.

I'm always trying to reinvent myself to stay relevant. Otherwise, by this time people start slowing down. After retirement, it is very tough to cope with the sudden loss of power and position that comes with your job. It can be difficult for most people, they kind of give up. Social media has given me a new life. It's like a new career for me. I always wore saris, I learned about them, but I didn't know that I knew so much about them. When I started writing, I discovered that I knew so much about handloom. People acquire that knowledge by reading books after books. Till date I have not read any book on this subject, including Geeta Kapoor Chishti's, purposely.

First, I want to write down whatever I know, whatever I have learnt during my saree journey. So, that is that. I don't know what's ahead of me.

You have held your own leadership style very distinctly in a patriarchal country. Any tips you would like to give to other women about the feminine style of leadership?
I would say women have to be themselves. Women don't have to be like men, there have been so many women leaders all

over the world. I never wanted to be like a man. I wanted to retain all my feminity because I wasn't ashamed of being a woman. I think my being a woman always helped me, I could do a very difficult job because I could reach out to people with my abilities, with my qualities with whatever God has given me as a woman, there are different attributes in a woman. I did it just the way I would do it. Women can lead, they have all the attributes to lead, to be successful as a leader or reach the top of any organization. It has to do with your abilities, your decision-making ability, your judgment, how you treat your team, you have to be a visionary to lead.

If you have all these attributes, it will show in your behaviour.

What is that "extra" they have? What is that which makes them right for leadership?
I think women have sharp intuition. Women are better in building and nurturing relationships. They are more magnanimous and compassionate because they manage their home, their family, extended one as well, which are bigger challenges than office. It starts at home. So, when you're managing so many people, why can't you manage your office? You take a lot of learnings about managing people from your home with you. You have to adjust so much with your help at home with the people around you, who help you to go to work. You learn compassion, you organize yourself, you empower others. I think women learn all these things while running their own house.

I also had brilliant male bosses from whom I learned how to run my office. It's not fair to say that women do it better than a man. You are just an Officer, either a good one or a bad one.

❝ My take on Vijayalaxmi

Her upbringing

When I read Vijayalaxmi's interview, I cannot help but notice the importance of culture and its symbols, language, food, and dress, in her scheme of things. Her passion for her beliefs shows up in her talk, and in her public persona. It is an attitude which was inculcated in her growing up. Because she has talked so much about her family, I get the feeling that education was and is the currency in their home. In business families, it is profit making, in music families it is music, in professional families it is education. And that currency makes the family so different in their way of living. It is this currency which differentiates people in India most clearly. Having lived in a particular currency makes people more suited to linked professions (Note for HR).

Her Career

It was refreshing to see that women have an advantage in AIR & Broadcasting. Rightly she says, it is to do with your abilities - decision-making, judgment, how you treat your team and, being a visionary. These are competencies which are not gender linked. Similarly, AIR & Doordarshan are skill-based organizations where gender did not impact the delivery of work. It comes with experience. There is no gender bias here.

Idealism, passion and execution distinguish her tenure as Director General in DD. It was heartening to see how these capabilities have taken nation building to the next level. It is also inspiring to read about her parents having done their part to take this country further. At a deeper level it is what has built continuity and growth of institutions.

Women specific
In context of feminization of the workplace, her golden words indicate that women have to work from their natural strengths and take a long-term view of their career. Through processes and structure, the next generation can take an inclusive ideology further, make it more encompassing and compelling.

As she says, women have a keenly honed intuition to make relationships as they have to manage a home. The woman is motivating people from different strata of society and making her family their priority. Home is the most important cog in every family member's wheel because the environment at home determines behavior outside the home, that is where children learn the most, about respect, kindness and being human. Parenting determines the emotional wellness of society.

One can see in Vijaya Jee's home hospitality, idealism, professional pursuit, financial independence and working for a larger national objective, as the lived values.

She calls Saree, power dressing. Being the most elegant, most versatile clothing for women. It makes wearer look stately, sober, sophisticated depending on the fabric. I am most heartened reading that.

Anita Khurana
COMMERCIAL DIRECTOR, AIR INDIA & INDIAN AIRLINES

A CHANCE CONVERSATION brought the 1st Lady of Commercial Aviation, Anita Khurana into pursuing an MBA, and a fancy for men in uniforms brought her to Indian Airlines as a career choice. For many years she lay low as she learnt the ropes. But once she decided to assert herself, her string of achievements took her to the top in record time! The list is long and impressive because she was having fun in her work:

- Passenger and Cargo Marketing in the National Airlines.
- Achieved motivational turnaround of Cargo Employees.
- Responsible for Complete turnaround in Cargo Division increasing sales by four-fold from USD 15 million (in 1994-95) to USD 55 million (in 1999-2000).
- Obtained ISO 9002 certification for Indian Airlines Cargo with UKAS and RAB Quality Accreditation of USA.
- Complete Automation of Cargo processes with online Tracking.
- Conversion of Boeing 737 passenger version aircraft into Freighters.
- Operation of Cargo Freighters from major Metros.
- Tie up with Department of Post for freighter operations to North Eastern Stations.

- Extensive Tie ups for offer of Domestic and International Holiday Packages.
- Introduction of innovative Sales schemes for passenger segment.
- Conceptualization and implementation of All India Centralized Call Center (24X7) help line with 150 work stations – a multilingual facility.
- Participated in IFCA International Contest wherein Indian Airlines won the Mercury Award 2002 (Silver Trophy) jointly presented by IFCA and IFSA (In-flight Service Association) for on board services
- Indian Airlines won PATWA award for Best Domestic Airlines in Marketing and Cuisine Services for two consecutive years, which were awarded at ITB Berlin.
- Achievement of winning Best Marketing person Awards
- Spearheading the Commercial department for merger activities between Indian Airlines and Air India.
- Retired as Board Member for the National Airlines – Air India.

Though her story reads like that of a serious achiever. I assure you talking to her is something else. So vivacious, with a laugh running throughout the narrative, she finished her interview in one breath, without losing any speed. And that she is a perfectionist is something I can vouch for. Her academics reflect where it comes from.

1. Stood 1st in Maharashtra Merit List of HSC School Exam.
2. Bachelor of Science with honors in Chemistry.
3. Recipient of National Science Talent Search Scholarship for Maths.
4. MBA (Masters of Management Studies) from Jamnalal Bajaj Institute of Management Studies, Mumbai with specialization in Marketing. Stood 1st in Marketing class.

5. Professional Education:- Lead Auditors Course for Quality Management.

Do not miss out on My Takeaways after finishing the interview.

Sat, 11/6 9:56PM • 1:30:21

Please tell us something about your family background. Let's start with your upbringing. Was it in a joint family or nuclear family? And was your dad in government service or a professional?

I belong to a North Indian Bania, nuclear family. My dad was in the army, and my mother was a homemaker. We are four children. I was the third in order.

Typically, in Bania families, "education" is the primary focus. Children can play as much as they want, but in class they have to 'Top'. Dad wanted us to do well in life, he was a great motivating factor. He was perfectly happy with my mom being at home, but he wanted his children to be self-dependent. There was a kind of an academic push. That was the environment that we grew up in, a middle-class family with total focus on education.

When I completed schooling, my mother passed away due to Cancer. I was just sixteen. Dad had to then devote himself to us. Till then, I had never participated in household chores and was under the impression that my elder sister will henceforth manage the house. But dad told me, "You have so far been enjoying yourself. Your elder sister is doing medical and I don't want her studies to be affected, so she's going to hostel. Now you have to take care of the house, as well as your younger brother". That came as a shock to me. It meant taking my responsibility from Zero to Hundred; and along with it, I had to continue with my studies.

What was the environment like, at home? Were your parents very strict? Were there any differences, as far as bringing up 'son versus daughter' is concerned?

My mom was a graduate but she was perfectly happy being a homemaker. She loved cooking, stitching, knitting, embroidery, and raising happy healthy kids. We never felt any difference in the treatment of 'son vs. daughter' because both my parents were very particular that they should treat all four of us the same. Mom just needed one person to help her in the kitchen. My sister was there and that was good enough. It was not like I was the daughter so I had to help in the kitchen. It was not like being treated differently at all but yes, in Bania society typically, there are differences in how a woman is treated vis a vis a man. Like you have to give dowry for daughter's wedding. I hated that part. When Dad would sit with us kids to have dinner at the table, my mom would serve us hot rotis. Then my mom would sit on the table while one of us would get up and make hot rotis for her. I never liked Mom not joining us for meals. But there were no pronounced messages around that, just a societal norm that we followed.

My husband's family was a little different. They were Punjabis and they would say that you ladies cook and then come to the table and then we will all eat together. Sometimes my husband would get up and make rotis for all of us. I saw that as a very clear difference between the two cultures.

In our house, we all were not only treated similarly both for education and career, but were also told that we have to be financially independent.

In school were you the hard-working child or the class prefect or the backbencher? And how did that shape you?

I was always the front bencher. My name was Anita Aggarwal, so roll number wise also I was first. Since all my siblings topped, I was always under pressure that even I have to do well. For me it was not always so easy, because my focus was on having fun at that time. I had to work hard.

As you know in a science class, you have the nerdy variety. For instance, as science students we would reach college at about 7 / 7.30 In the morning, for four to five hours we'd be doing experiments in the chemistry lab. After that, we would go for lecture sessions. Around that time, we would see arts and commerce students arriving, looking very smart, with their freshly blow-dried hair. Guys would be after these smart girls, but for notes the same guys would come around asking me. Those were fun moments. I genuinely loved studying there. Professors were very nice and I had a good group of friends.

Did you take part in any debate or sports or any other activities besides studies?
I participated in dramatics in school. I was tall so it was easy to be selected for dance or drama. I was very good in Sanskrit so was in selected even for a Sanskrit play. Besides that, I played Badminton and Table Tennis.

Which school and college did you study from?
I did my schooling from Kendriya Vidyalaya, IIT Powai and passed B. Sc. (honours) in Chemistry from Jai Hind College, Mumbai.

Were there any influences from your college days, which impacted your choice of profession? Gender specific ones particularly. Was there any particular incident you can recall?
Nothing in BSc whatsoever. The only thing was that, I was pursuing a subject which was very close to my heart. I didn't mind pursuing it provided it gave me a good career opportunity after doing a postgraduation. But it limited my options. At the most, you can end up as a professor or lecturer in a college which did not interest or excite me. I couldn't fancy myself teaching. I wanted my parents to be proud of

me. From a social perspective, you want to be a somebody and make a good career choice. I mean, doing MBA never came to my mind.

Only thing I felt was that now it will be time to get married and parents will start talking about marriage. If I did B.Sc. Home Science, I could be a good housewife. I loved cooking, embroidery, stitching, Ikebana etc. I guess I inherited these likings from my mom. I still do. It was a different kind of mindset at that time.

But you ended up doing MBA. Can you just take us through your choice of MBA as a career?
It's all because of a family member who asked me," Why do you want to do home science? You are managing the house pretty well on your own. That means you can be a good professional manager". As a result of his counselling, I applied for MBA at JBIMS and I got selected. That's how my journey began. I didn't have any ambition or such goals about reaching any career level. I was living in a world of my own, just coping with too many things happening around me at that time. But once I joined MBA my world changed drastically.

After MBA how did the transition into that serious career minded woman, happen?
In the first year of MBA, frankly, I was totally lost because my earlier chosen science stream was very systematic with an organized way of dealing with things. Here in the first year, we had all kinds of subjects like economics, commerce, business law subjects that were not in my horizon at all. These were new and difficult for me to understand. We had students from different backgrounds - arts, commerce, engineering, chartered accountancy etc. who were very open to sharing their perspective. They were vocal whereas I think I was a little timid and shy to speak up my mind. So, in the first year, I felt pretty much out of place. But it was a great learning time for

me because I was observing, seeing how people are, preparing myself for working with people in the future. I realized that there is more to life than the exposure I had had so far. To be a success, you need to know that there are all kinds of people whom you will meet and be friends with. It's a competitive world. I had this realization that I am a frog out of a well and that I need to find my place in this world.

In the second year, we had to choose a specialization. I chose 'marketing' as my main subject. That was great fun. It was drastically different. In the first year I remember wearing traditional clothes - salwar kurta, walking with my head down, my hair in a plait till my waist. By the end of the first year, I decided this is not the way to survive in a man's world. So, I cut my hair, switched to Bell Bottoms and tops.

Marketing was an enjoyable subject. We were only five girls, and a majority of guys in class, but there was a very nice atmosphere. Jamnalal Bajaj was one of the finest institutes. We had projects to be done which meant that we travelled everywhere, made questionnaires, interviewed and prepared project reports. That was a great learning experience, challenging, yet very enjoyable.

You were picked up by Indian Airlines during your placement. Was that a conscious choice, something you wanted?
In Bajaj the engineers were the first persons to get picked. They were the first ones to get all the plum jobs. After that were the science students. Arts and commerce were preferred for Finance and personnel management jobs. I had another project in the second year which was marketing of saris. Two Saree companies - Mafatlal and Bombay Dyeing were in the fray. I had 5 jobs to choose from. Though Indian Airlines was not paying as well as the others, I chose Indian Airlines because of my love for the uniform. Dad used to wear his army uniform all shiny and smart. He was very proud of his

uniform. I thought I'll get to wear a nice uniform as well. At the airport you would see those pilots and air hostesses smartly turned out in uniform. No doubt it was a flimsy kind of a thought process to choose a job, but that's what appealed to me at that time.

Since Aviation was a very small industry at that time, did it ever hinder your job opportunities in the market?
No, I did not think of that. I did think that since I would be required to travel from place to place, I would need flexibility. I had no clue about what placement entailed or the transfer requirements of Indian Airlines. The only thought was that I am completing my post-graduation and getting into a job, so I have to like what I'm doing. Once I have some experience, I will take a call as to any other opportunity that arises within the company.

Once the basic foundation is laid, you can market any service OR product. As a professional, whatever you learn, you can assimilate and use it wherever it may apply. Only Marketing strategy needs to change for different products or services.

What advice would you give to women when they choose a career?
Looking back, I think women have to have that little stability in their job as a requirement unless a person says I don't want to get married, or that I'm not going to have kids, or that I don't want to run a family, or that I just want to be a single career person. Many women have that mindset nowadays, in fact more so than in our time. So, for such women I can think there are many more career opportunities to jump into besides managing her house, children, food, family's well-being, and travelling. Women need to handle role conflicts that continuously evolve. A positive attitude always helps to deal with them.

'Marriage & Career; or Marriage vs Career? Do you think one has to sacrifice their career for marriage? Does marriage have anything to do with feeling fulfilled in life? I'm a bit of a feminist. I'm strongly in favor of women working and being on their own, being self-dependent, confident and being able to sustain themselves through marriage and career.

Women have to think about family also because you wouldn't want a job situation ending up becoming a role conflict. Not so much for men, but woman's role in the family changes the moment they start a family. They want to be with the children and do their best for them.

We are naturally attuned to positioning ourselves as the caretakers of the family. It is somewhere in our head that "it is our job" though it is not necessarily so. It is a shared job for both husband and wife, where both of them are working professionals.

Women need to learn to delegate responsibilities and get as much support as possible. They have to look after themselves. But at the same time amongst the two partners, there must be a good understanding. So, girls should choose their partner with great care. That definitely is a basic requirement.

At this stage I would suggest girls to hire domestic help or baby sitters. When you are earning, you can afford to spend your earnings on these kinds of support requirements specific to you. This helps you perform better, especially if your children are young. But you need to focus on career. If you do everything yourself then you will not be able to do justice to your career. You can't say okay I will stop this and take a break in my career while you are a beginner or let me take a break and catch up with career when my kids are big enough. No, you have to manage both the things.

There's a lot to be done to maintain work, home and life balance. In the Indian environment especially, if you have only a single common account of both your earnings, it can become difficult, as it can create a point of friction at a later point. You contribute to some common household expenditure but keep a little bit of financial independence in your hands so you can do your own things. Needs and wants are different for a man and a woman. You may want to dress up and look good.

Every woman, I feel, must get married because there's a different kind of joy to be enjoyed together, share companionship and have children.

Did you get any professional training in your career? What were the challenges you faced?
Indian Airlines is a semi government organization. It had a feel of both government as well as private sector culture. It had a lot of flexibility. At the point of time when I joined, the airlines had very recently started hiring personnel at 'Management' level whom they took as trainees. We were actually the fifth batch who had joined as 'management trainees'. There was another batch of officers who had joined much before I did. Even the staff were very skeptical about having a 'young inexperienced manager' in their vicinity and that too, a lady, to have come as their boss and to call her 'Ma'am' was a little bit too much for them to take, or so it seemed.

It was challenging from the beginning, to be accepted. In the entire Western region, Indian Airlines did not have a single management trainee before me. Being the first management trainee, everybody would look at me with apprehension, whether this young, inexperienced girl would be able to manage.

At that point, I was well versed with my marketing fundamentals, but had no clue about the procedures of basic airline activities like: how to issue a ticket, make reservations and other operational activities. I knew how important it was for me to win everybody's heart, to be a good manager and be humble at the same time. I tried to come at par to their level of learning and expertise by understanding them instead of dominating them. One thing was crystal clear, and that was they had more experience than me. It is rightly said that 'experience' teaches the young to be old and the old to be young. Besides trying to learn job from them and to gain respect and confidence of my staff I adopted the all favourite, formal dress code- saree. A Saree is a lot more graceful and gives you more credibility. This helped me win everybody's respect and I am thankful for it and felt on top of the world. My appearance said out loud in not so many words, "I may be your manager but I am down to earth."

So, to win people's confidence and to win their trust, was I think my first challenge which I overcame.

One thing MBA does to you is it makes you feel that you are a 'CEO', who has been freshly minted out of a factory; where you can take all decisions. You can control everybody and your word is a command. In real life things are pretty much the opposite. The reality being, you're just a nobody. It is like being a drop in a vast ocean. Such is the nature of the corporate world around us.

That was my second challenge.

So, I started with a market research exercise to find out if there was 'business potential' for the Airline. My boss was open to experimenting with me. Thankfully, it worked out fine. In Mumbai, there was never any discrimination.

After marriage, I shifted to Delhi. Delhi, being the hub of politics, got to me. This is where the 'Man – Woman' divide comes in. As compared to Delhi, Mumbai was very open and so in Delhi I felt like a stranger, thrown in towards the deep end of the ocean, amongst politically savvy men and women.

By then my son was born and I could manage well, because ours was a joint family. It was a personal life change for me as well as a cultural change in office. To handle that, I needed to be settled both at home and at office. Slowly I overcame my third challenge as well – of managing work and family.

At this time, I decided to lie low, till my second child was born. By the time I had my second child, the men had already played their politics and I found myself transferred to cargo marketing in the airline.

To give you a feel of the cargo division, for any full-service passenger carrier, Passenger division is the basic revenue earner. It is the glamorous part of working - meeting passengers, doing proper marketing, sales. The Cargo operations on the other hand, take a backseat, accounting for only five percent of the airlines' revenue. After passenger seats are filled up, any cargo hold left is what you are supposed to market. Moreover, in the cargo division, the staff deputed are the undesirable ones, who can't work anywhere else. The ones who are totally demotivated and distracted. You can imagine what being 'Head' of such a department would feel like. It was a very demotivating situation for me.

There were many problems too, major being-how to sell without proper motivated manpower. I somehow gathered up courage and indulged in self-motivation. Deciding to take it as a challenge, I found myself looking at it like an opportunity. It was time to show my mettle. That became a turning point in my career. The cargo division emerged as the prominent division and left the passenger division behind. Now staff wanted to be in the cargo division.

There were a series of actions I took, that got noticed. I realized I was now in the limelight. This period of my career gave me immense job satisfaction, for, I had managed a 'turnaround', without much resources at my disposal.

Can you brief us on some of the management actions you took which catapulted you to a Board Directorship?
It started with when I took over the Cargo division. It was disheartening to see the pathetic condition of the infrastructure of the cargo division in Delhi. One could mostly see broken chairs and a leaking roof. So, I wracked my brains to bring out a plan in order to improve the entire scenario of that

division. I organized a competition amongst the staff of Delhi, Bombay, Calcutta, Chennai, Hyderabad and Bangalore with lucrative accolades. Attractive posters, stickers, brochures and Cargo friendly utility gifts were ordered utilizing the 'marketing budget'. Visits of local cargo offices were organized every month to judge the cargo premises, based on certain basic parameters like cleanliness, manning of the counters, complete turnout in uniform and display of posters etc., by certain officers. Promotional stickers were used to hide the broken portions of the chairs and posters were stuck to hide the damaged walls.

This initiative worked like Harry Potter's magic wand. The outcome being allocation of funds for the cargo division – something that had never happened before. History was created, as the Directors and the CMD started visiting the Cargo section to see how everything had changed. The staff was now motivated enough to work in a neat and clean environment. Brochures, posters were sent to the entire network as a goodwill gesture with gifts for loyal customers. The clients were happier, they came to a neater place, and received better services provided by a more enthusiastic staff. Another benchmark was the ISO quality certification for cargo unit.

Till then we operated on manual mode. It took me 13 long years to get cargo operations automated overcoming internal politics and paucity of funds. But I persisted. Not to mention the basic English fundamentals and the computer training that the staff had to undergo.

How I prepared my so called 'sales force' is worth mentioning. The top management at Regional Cargo units was reluctant to spare extra workers. All I got was ten people who were supposed to be non-performers as per their boss's perspective. After much ado they were welcomed to my 'special sales team', saying that they had been cherry picked. This took them by surprise. Each one of them gave fairly decent suggestions, certainly not the best but some of them were worth implementing. After having them groomed at the airhostess' grooming centre in Hyderabad – (table manners, dressing, hygiene, cleanliness, walking etc.), got kits ordered– (shaving cream and lotion, perfume, the basics). Nobody would believe their eyes if they saw them before and after training. They had had a complete transformation of sorts, in just a span of seven days.

Now the department had a formal sales process with a proper Sales Manual and Cargo managers now had somebody to help them. The department started attracting Staff. In fact, people found it lucrative to work as a part of the sales team. But I wouldn't let them in unless they proved themselves. After all, there was a reputation to maintain.

It was a very exciting phase and everything worked out fine.

Much later in my career, I was allocated five Boeing 737 aircraft, which were not wanted by the Airlines. I got them converted into freighters. We started freighter services between five stations in the country. It was out of the box thinking, a first for the country and the airline.

The most challenging assignment in the passenger division that I did was creating a 24x7 call centre for the airline. Earlier the procedure was a cumbersome one. I was expected to start a call centre with a single number for passengers, from scratch. I started researching, reading and getting to know about its implementation. I learnt about call centres, created an RFP with a great deal of perseverance and hard work. Finally, a 100-seater Call Centre was created, and that too in eight languages. A single telephone number was available 24X7. Even though, it was implemented in phases, it gave me complete sense of fulfilment. Again, it was a first for the airline.

For passengers in the south, I introduced Tamil and Malayalam languages. First, I myself tried to understand that language, made an FAQ which was in English, converted

FAQs into local language. and ensured that right training was given to call centre agents of that particular language. In some time, dialect issues were solved. For me, it was an absolute passion. At the end of the day, it is job satisfaction that matters.

Having worked in public sector company was there anything about the Indian culture which hindered you, from a woman's perspective?

Even when the board vacancy position was announced, there were so many of us Directors who were eligible. It was the first time the company was planning to appoint Directors in our Board from outside the ministry. Most of my director friends, ladies, senior directors did not apply. They believed that nothing will come out of it. I applied, just to experience the process. First time I didn't get selected but I was on priority number two. Priority number one was a director senior to me. So, he got to be the Board Director. When second time it came, I was priority number one so I was selected. Around the same time the merger happened between Air India and Indian Airlines and I came on the Board of the combined entity Air India. At the same time my batch mates from JBIMS who were with Air India earlier, overnight became my juniors while I was junior to them in college. This led to a lot of resentment and politics. As it is, Air India and Indian Airlines were two different companies, with different mindsets. To have somebody who was junior to them in JBIMS, to be their boss, led to further complications. Similarly, colleagues in my company who were senior to me as directors, couldn't digest that I was a Board Director whereas they had not even applied for the post.

This came out in the form of snide comments, which were still tolerable. But then when they would all get together and started politicizing, it was very hurtful. Last couple of years in my career I wasn't very happy because of the internal politics. But other than that, I thought my career had been satisfying and great as I had been able to face all challenges.

In my late 30's, I lost my husband in an air crash so I had to also look after my two children to make sure their studies are not affected. There were a lot of things happening in my personal life adding to the work place complications.

One thing I hated was politicizing but that is a given in a corporate job whether it is a man or woman. Politics affects both genders equally.

"My take on
Anita Khurana

Her Career
If every loss-making PSU had one Anita in its midst, it would not be loss-making at all. Anita was the first lady Commercial Director of Air India, a feat she achieved for a long list of initiatives she successfully undertook - Cargo turnaround, Freighter ops, Call centre, which showcased her managerial capability. It is also an outcome of her living the value of Meritocracy, which prompted her to apply for the position. Everything she has handled has been laced with passion and being open to challenges life has thrown at her.

Leadership
She is truly a people leader, achieving the turnaround of cargo division by revitalizing the team she had been given. One can see how much she has enjoyed her work and making her teams feel good about themselves.
She makes it sound so easy – no networking, no flashy stories just good ol' motivation, making people feel good about their jobs, her humility, and her no-nonsense approach. It is loads of sense of humour which ensured that the highly charged culture of Delhi did not faze her.

Her upbringing
It came from the push at home to excel in studies and do

well in life which has translated into healthy competition with peers. You see that competitive streak in her in college and at work as well. Her mother's passing away when she was a teenager and her father giving her the household responsibility along with studies taught her the valuable lesson of responsibility and adapting to that.

The value of self-sufficiency learnt from parents has ensured that she continued with her job even after she lost her husband.

Women specific

Anita shows women the way to be self-dependent – selecting our partner with great care, delegating housework, keeping some part of our earning separate, not taking breaks from work to manage the basic challenges of being a working mom, or rather handle "our job" without compromising on our career. And lastly pointing out the stability which career moms need in their work if they want to avoid a role conflict.

Anita has brought up the topic of role conflict, which continuously evolves. Before the sentence dissappears in translation, this is the biggest challenge married women face; how to transition between an ideal wife, mother and daughter-in-law at home and an assertive worker at the workplace. If we can find a solution to this, we can stem the tide of women leaving the workplace. This is a good career related insight.

This is the best piece of career related advice I have received till now.

Panchali Upadhaya
VICE PRESIDENT S & M, HERBALIFE

THE CLIMB UP the ladder has not been easy for Panchali. How she has worked on herself, to get the business head positions she so deserved. Unlike a guy, a woman has to "prove" that she is "capable". A to-be employer has every right to decide on candidate, but sometimes professional head hunters who act like gate keepers and decide whether the woman deserves to be considered. This is what Panchali has had to face in the past, while she quietly changed the stereotype of the Business leader to that of a soft-spoken leader.

Her experience across industry verticals like E-commerce, medical devices, fashion, Beauty and Retail stands testimony to her versatility as a business leader. She has a proven track record in setting up new business units, delivering results across Commercial Operations, Marketing and Sales to drive growth for Global and leading Indian brands. Her strong leadership skills in establishing and developing high performing teams are all learned skills, honed over the years.

Here is a bird's eye view of her experience:
- ❖ Herbalife, 2023 – Currently Vice President Sales and Marketing

- Alcon, 2017- 2023 - Country Franchise Head, Global Director
- Flipkart, 2015-2017- Senior Director
- VF India, 2008 - 2013 Business Head
- Trent Ltd. (Tata Group) - 2005 - 2008 (3 years) Head New II 1999 – 2004 Manager Communication & Research
- Cussons India, 1995 - 1999 Brand Manager for "Imperial Leather" and "Ezee"
- DCM Shriram, Management Trainee

Her professional qualifications have given her a foot in the door, but it is the drive to improve herself that has taken her to the top.

1. Institute of Management Development and Research (IMDR), Pune Post Graduate in Management
2. Poona University - Bachelor in Arts (Economics)

Monday, 01/ 03 2022

Tell us something about your upbringing. Were you brought up in a joint family or nuclear? Was your father in government service, private job or family business?

I grew up in a middle/upper middle-class family in the 70s and 80s. My father came from a large joint family. The family was very progressive. My father was employed with the government and I largely grew up in cantonments. My mother was a homemaker who grew up in a nuclear family.

My schooling was in multiple cities, Lucknow and Calcutta being the primary ones. Five years of my college life was in Pune and I started my work life in Delhi.

What was the environment like at home? Were your parents very strict? Were there any differences as far as bringing up 'son versus daughter' is concerned?
I came from a pretty liberal family. My parents were both easy-going, so I can't say it was strict. I think they were probably stricter for my brother because he used to get into a lot of scrapes, but I was generally one of those quiet children who would get 'good conduct' certificates in school. I think it was pretty peaceful in that sense. Both my parents were big readers, who encouraged me to read. I have fond memories of spending Sunday mornings at the library with my father. We grew up in the times of 'Doordarshan' and TV time was limited.

I don't think the way I was brought up was any different from my brother. We were both free to make our choices and decide on our paths, what we wanted to study, what we wanted to do. There was never any sort of restrictions around it and there was a lot of encouragement.

The expectation was that you would go to a good college. I went to an average one but they continued to be supportive.

I've always been a very, shy person. But 'that's just me', It's not my environment. I'm privileged that I come from a family that encouraged me & wanted me to do well.

Who were you in school, the teacher's pet, the class bully or the mouse? And how did that shape you?
I'm trying to remember now. I went to multiple schools, because of the nature of my father's job. Every new school takes time to settle down. It's not easy. Teachers liked me, because I was one of those non problematic kids. I did my work, kept quiet and was better than average in studies.

Once I started working, it took me a lot of work to actually move forward and start expressing myself. But earlier I would not be the first one to come and volunteer for something in college or be a part of popular groups. Individual interactions however were never difficult for me, though.

In any organization, you need to be able to network, negotiate and push forward. I had to really push myself on this. It still does not come to me naturally. My natural tendency would be to be quiet and blend in.

Did you go for any training programs to overcome that?
Over a period of time, I have had help from my organizations in terms of coaching or mentoring. That really helped. I wish I had access to it much earlier in my career.

I also worked around it with more preparation and practicing with what I wanted to present. Since communication is not only about "how" but also about "what". That approach helped me immensely.

Don't you think that it is organization's loss if they are unable to differentiate between a quiet performer and a more talkative one?
Let's be clear. Most of us are not spectacular. But, you know, there is only that much difference, maybe 20% or 15%, or 10%, if appraised objectively.

Suppose I'm a manager, and I'm doing my calibration. The data has to guide you.

I remember something my coach told me; Leaders remember only 5 percent of the people. You have to work to be part of that 5%. You have to make an effort to know - who are the influencers? Who are going to make a difference in a career? And how do they think about me? What is it that I want them to think about me? How am I going about it? Who has positive opinions, who has negative opinions, who has no opinions?

Any influences from your college days, which impacted your choice of profession? Gender specific ones particularly. Was there any particular incident that you can recall?
A bit of both actually. I knew what I did not want to do. I knew I was going to have a corporate career. It was really important that I feel respected, that I manage my own money and that I'm not dependent on anybody. But within that, there was no calling as such. I enjoyed HR and specialized in it because I wanted to be in training and development. I did my summer project in Industrial Relations at TOMCO. But I could not land a T&D job.

After my post-graduation I did some academic work with the National Institute of Bank Management but I realized academics was not for me.

So, I started looking at other things. I applied through an ad for the Management Trainee program with DCM Sriram. I got a lot of free hand there as it was a small consumer product within a largely B2B company. I got to do a whole lot more than what I would have done in a regular marketing organization.

Where did you acquire your professional education and training?
I got my MBA from Institute of Management Development and Research (IMDR) Pune.

Like most people I learned on the job. I have learnt from my peers, managers, agencies, vendors, distributors and the larger eco system. When you start out you are just absorbing things all around. For me it continues to this day.

Increasingly I think I am learning the most from my teams. It is a continuous process.

I have been lucky to have managers who have given me a free hand, driven me hard and allowed me to make mistakes. I have had some brilliant managers.

Having worked in both MNCs and Indian companies was there anything about the Indian culture which hindered you, from a woman's perspective?
I don't know, whether it's Indian versus multinational, or because times have changed. I have worked for very progressive Indian companies. I see the change over the years.

Organization now encourage / pushes you to develop your women talent. Managers have to answer for diversity rating. There is a pressure in the system. This is an index that you carry at the highest level.

But having said that, how much of it is happening down the line?

For example, it's a challenge in sales organizations, I don't see enough women. There are real physical barriers. Sales people travel a lot. At junior level, travel is not as comfortable. If you're in the sales team, you're taking a bus or train, so it is more difficult for a woman. In one of my previous team there were several lady medical reps and who were doing extremely well, because of supportive managers. Attitudes are changing.

I remember a funny incident from early in my career. I went to meet a distributor in Mysore and he didn't know what to do with me. Started showing me a family album. Now it is quite common to have women in these roles.

Infrastructures have improved, which helps. Today if you're working in a small town, you have a coffee shop or a mall where you can walk in and use the loo. Small towns now have so many decent hotels. The mid-tier hotels were missing in India. The ecosystem and infrastructure of the country is changing, which helps.

In your career domain, were you mentored by anybody?
I don't think I ever asked for mentoring. Not till much later in my life. I have learned a lot from my managers early on in my career. They have pushed me and have believed that I could do better.

I have had access to coaches and mentors for some time now and it really helps.

In career were you at any time tempted to change your industry track?
I have actually changed many industries. I have worked across retail, lifestyle brands, Ecommerce, medical devices and nutrition. I have changed industries throughout.

I enjoyed the challenge of learning new things. I like the change; I like the challenge of the change.

In your opinion, what is the common mistakes made by most working women?
Not staying on in the workforce. Women give up too early, they drop out. They need to be pushing more, fighting more. It tends to happen more when your children are young, it's difficult to manage. It becomes difficult to come back into the workforce. I think the organizations need to be more open to taking women back into the workforce at different stages of their lives. It's becoming more and more open. But I always say that even if you're not able to do this full time try to stay on in the workforce. I see so many talented women drop out of the workforce.

What about marriage and careers? Do you think both can mix? Do you think that marriage is important to feel fulfilled?
I don't think there is a conflict at all. Obviously, you and your partner have to be clear about what your career aspirations are, and have a mutual respect for each other. I can speak from my personal experience; it was never at conflict. Obviously, situations are different for each person.

Getting married is a very personal thing. For somebody, it might be important, somebody it may not be. They might be equally fulfilled, unmarried. You have to make that choice for yourself.

How can women ensure that their voice gets heard?
If you really have something important to say, your manager does listen to you. If you have a point of view, be firm and clear about it. Sometimes if you feel that in a room, you were not heard then send out a mail later, saying this was my point of view, we never came around to discussing it, but I wanted to express it. If you really have an opinion which matters, it will be heard.

Be clear, be firm and express yourself.

What do you have to say about dress? What do you think is a good professional dress code for women?
In a professional environment normally, people dress smartly. It's about the industry you're from, and what is the norm of the industry. Dressing is a way of expressing yourself, and you are free to express yourself any way you like.

What motivates you? How do you renew yourself?
I have a fairly balanced life. I don't think it is all about work

though work does take up a lot of my time. I love to read. Reading is a form of relaxation for me, and it's been all my life. I socialize, I go out, spend time with family. I love to plan for the holidays about twice a year.

From whom did you imbibe your early leadership lessons? And what was that? Did you go for any courses as such?
I think I have worked with some fabulous leaders, and I've seen the way they handle situations. Having a very clear vision and goal and *why* we are trying to achieve something, is important. To be able to communicate that and making sure it sort of becomes a common narrative for the organization, that's what has helped me.

If I'm talking about team management, my style comes from a space of empathy. I've always tried to hear people out and understand the challenges they face, try to put myself in that space and see if I can find solutions. Now, having said that, even if there is empathy, you still need to deliver on the organization's goals. There is no one right style of leadership, there are multiple ways. It has been mine and it seems to have worked for me.

What about your peers, how would you like to be remembered by them?
I'd like to be seen as a strong leader who comes from a place of empathy, a strong 'people' leader, a strong business leader.

Looking back, is there something you would have liked to do differently?
I think I should have been more confident and vocal about my work. It is not just important to do good work but also to ensure your work is visible. You need to truly believe in

yourself and stand up for what you deserve.

I should have also networked more. It does not come naturally to me but I think this is very important for career growth.

"My take on Panchali

Her Career

If I look at Panchali's resume, I see a life statement. Every company is a 3-to-5-year tenure, every new job is a step up. But most refreshing is her honesty about her shortcomings which reflects her vulnerability and her secret to growth. Looking at her CV any youngster can take away the lesson that while you cannot choose your first job, you can certainly choose thereafter. Only in your first job you can choose to appear ignorant and wait for somebody to teach you or do the work, learn from the mistakes. That is called "experience".

The thing that strikes me most about Panchali is her determination and her willingness to learn. For e.g., from Sheryl Sandberg she has imbibed "raising your hand, knowing about your self-worth, I think that was missing in me and that did hinder my career for a while".

Leadership

Panchali has a very objective process for assessing people, which has been honed with experience. Being a quiet person, one tends to listen and observe more. No doubt that's what makes her more empathetic. Moderated by her business-like approach, she would be a good role model for women aspiring to balance their intuitiveness with their business accountability.

As a business leader who has grown on the strength of her hard work rather than an "old boys" club, there must be a constant pressure on her to perform. The fact that she is grown in each of her role is testimony to the fact that she has delivered. It underlines the need for women to have strong communication to align them to organization's vision, mission, without bringing your family into it.

Kre'sha Bajaj
CREATIVE DIRECTOR 'KOESHE'

CREATIVE DIRECTOR, KRE'SHA Bajaj is no stranger to the fashion world, with over 15 years of experience. She hails from a family that has pioneered bespoke wear. At the tender age of 4, KRE'SHA started sketching ideas, when most children were outdoors playing; KRE'SHA's playground was her father's tailoring shop. To channel this passion, she decided to study the technicalities of fashion. Over a span of 8 years, she studied in some of the world's most distinguished fashion colleges including London College of Fashion, Parsons in New York and Paris and Fashion Institute of Design & Merchandising in Los Angeles, before deciding to return home to Mumbai. Diving into the industry head on, KRE'SHA launched her e-commerce website, Koëcsh, a brand with no name or face associated to it. She was soon invited to showcase her collection at Lakme Fashion Week, which garnered a lot of appreciation for being avant-garde and unique. As the years passed by, her designs started to evolve as did she.

After a long, grueling experience looking for bridal wear, she decided to create her own wedding outfits. Looking back at her relationship with her fiancé (now husband) and how they met, she wanted to share their love story and what better way than to make it permanent on her wedding lehenga, fondly known as "the love story lehenga." Having garnered a lot of attention worldwide around her bridal lehenga, with her experience and knowledge, KRE'SHA decided to create bridal collections for what she discovered that real women want: effortless and fresh wearable pieces delivered with impeccable craftsmanship. The birth of KRE'SHA Bajaj the brand- from fabrics to embroidery and textures to colours, each piece of clothing tells its own story with the utmost care in detailing and finishing. A perfectionist with a fine eye for beautiful things, Kre'sha aims to maintain a standard that will be timeless.

KRE'SHA takes inspiration from the places she travels and people she meets but her outlook goes a step further, which shows clearly in her work. Her inspiration is recorded, pictures are taken, and she tries to capture the spirit and feelings of a location. These images are a starting point to source fabric that emulate the colour scheme and the theme, that will eventually be seen in her next collection. To capture the natural beauty, sensuality, freedom and given her process - her pieces seem to carry a significant weight - they tell a story. "Travels have always been a great influence on me as a creator" says KRE'SHA.

KRE'SHA's commitment to her patron is what makes the brand all the more special - she wants to give girls and women an intimate experience, one where they personally feel connected to the brand. And the brand aims at giving women a deep sense of pride in femininity, honoring women to feel comfortable and confident by wearing bold and beautiful silhouettes.

Kriesha Bajaj the store launched in Bandra in November 2018; an ode to all things beautiful, mysterious with a splash of fantasy.

Clothes are an essential part of the way a woman expresses herself, as a mother, a goddess, or a wife, a prime minister, an NGO worker or a courtesan. That's why this book has a question on dress, because the way they dress is an expression of who she wants to be. That's why the interview with Ms. Chabbra and Mrs KRE'SHA Bajaj weaves so beautifully into the essence of this book.

Over to KRE'SHA on her career story:

Interview Sat, 11/6 9:55PM • 5:22

Which part of the country do people with the surname 'Bajaj' hail from – Rajasthan or Punjab? Did you grow up in a joint or a nuclear family?
We are Sindhis. My grandparents migrated from Pakistan during the partition. Ours is a nuclear family, it has just been my parents and us growing up. I have a sister who's five years younger to me and a brother who is six years younger.

My dad started his own tailoring shop at the age of 16 or 17. He was very passionate about fashion and fashion designing. He discontinued his studies and went off on his own to start his brand Badasaab. His father was not too happy about this decision of his.

What was the environment like, at home? Was it very traditional? Were there any differences, as far as bringing up a son versus daughter is concerned?
I think both my parents are very different. My mom is very calm, chilled out and quite laid back. On the other hand, my dad was very strict. But when I say strict it was always to do with 'following of the rules' punctuality, honesty and integrity. You

will always find his wardrobe in a perfect condition, with his clothes and personal items all folded perfectly and organized by color. That means that we had to follow strict rules as far as organization of things, laying down curfew timings, setting of deadlines etc. But at the same time, he was a family-oriented parent, as all parents are. They were always by our side, whether it was a school play, sports day, or anything under the sun. They were extremely involved in our day-to-day life. We had to sit down every single day for our meals, together, be it breakfast or dinner. So, I would say, our upbringing was done meticulously, with love and understanding on one hand and respect for discipline, on the other.

In my case, I was actually treated like a boy because I was the firstborn child.

My parents have always been a little more western in their thinking, although they are traditional, in some matters. Many of my girlfriends had to go through the age-old process of an 'arranged marriage', which lays special emphasis on horoscope, caste and background of the spouse. But luckily for me, I didn't have to go through all that.

Did your family back ground affect your professional choices?
Yes, definitely. When I came into the system, both my parents were in this profession. My mom had a boutique called "First Lady" which she had to shut down due to health issues, in order to conceive. Dad had Badasaab. A few years later, Mom brought the first 'Benetton store' to India. I was kind of thrown into this. I remember my childhood days, after school, I would either go and sit at my mom's or dad's store. I would love to sit with the tailors and designers, to sketch. I would collect scraps of fabric to make coasters and mats. I

would then organize a Diwali sale or a Valentine's Day sale. So I think from the word 'go', I knew that I wanted to be in the creative field. Even in the evening, when I used to come home from school, instead of going down and playing with the rest of the building kids, I would be up, sitting with my crayons. It was at the age of four that I first drew. My first drawing was that of a cloud, the reason being I was obsessed to go to the cloud. I think I essentially had 'designing' in my blood and that was what I wanted to do.

Was it a family thing? What about your brother and sister. Were they also influenced by fashion and designing?
No, not at all. Actually my sister was running a few fine dining restaurants so she is in the Food and Beverage business. My brother along with real estate during the lockdown branched out into a wellness clinic called Reviv which specializes in IV (Intravenous) therapies. Anytime you will ask my dad, he will say, I have a daughter who is neck deep in fashion, my other daughter in food and son in Real Estate. Jokingly he said they are in 'Roti Kapda Makaan'.

So what was school life like? Who were you in school - The teacher's pet, the class bully or mouse or the back bencher? How did that shape you?
To be very honest, I went through different roles in different stages of my life. Primary school was very inclusive. Classes were very small; we would call our teachers 'Auntie'. We were not supposed to call them 'Ma'am'. It was a very happy space. I genuinely loved my teachers and they loved me too.

Around the fourth or fifth grade, I had to switch schools because my previous school ended at the fourth grade. There were issues settling down in this new school because girls and boys were not allowed to talk to each other. Other students would make fun of you if you spoke to boys. I was very talkative with the boys, as well. The boys actually were quite vocal and friendly. So somewhere down the line, the other girls started bullying me. At that point, my grades started to go down. I would come home and cry for hours, as they would play silly pranks on me, like they would put Fevicol in my hair or put something on my seat before I sat. Luckily for me, my parents decided to put me in a boarding school because the existing school didn't have a playground.

Eventually I went to Good Shepherd's in Ooty. It was an amazing and enriching experience, as it had many activities. I was part of the band and also took part in gymnastics. In some ways, they were also very conservative. The girls would sit in the front, the guys would sit at the back. I think the one thing that really saved me from becoming rebellious was how well I was doing there. I became a 'Prefect' and as a result learnt how to carry responsibility.

Thanks to that experience, I don't let anyone bully me or play pranks on me, anymore. I don't tolerate that kind of behaviour, whether it is from friends, family, clients or my team.

Where did you get your graduation degree from? Was the education and training abroad relevant in your practice here?
I studied in 4 different universities, starting from London College of Fashion. After that I moved on, to Parson's New York, 'Parson's Paris fashion', where I did my internship. Finally, I finished in the Fashion Institute of Design and Merchandising in Los Angeles.

At home my training was built on whatever was being

stitched at home, or in other words, whatever my mum was making. But that training was limited. I understood the basic formula of doing this business - how the karigars stitched, but in terms of that 'technical training', that you need only came through my education in the above-mentioned institutes.

Though I don't think any amount of training or education can give you the experience, that the real world does. However, because my father was in fashion, there were many things about the business that he had to figure out the hard way. Nothing is easy in life. At the start of his career, because of the lack of technical knowledge and training, he had to face many hardships. Moreover, he is not really a tech savvy person. He struggles with a laptop even today. Opening emails is not easy for him. So the one thing he told me was that, fashion can come across like a flamboyant profession, it can come across like you just need to put something out, you have a team of people to make it, but that's not what it is going to be. In the fashion industry, it's important for you to learn every single aspect of it. It's not kid's stuff. That's why my education is probably like three times more than the rest of my friends.

I studied fashion for eight years, I studied in different universities, everything from sketching to stitching to pattern, the marketing photography etc. So basically, I have studied every possible thing, under the fashion category. So now I am a confident business woman, really not dependent on anyone else to give me inputs, in order to get a finished product, out. Of course, I do have a team of Karigars, tailors and artisans, but I am not dependent on them. I can actually sit down and do it, all by myself.

In these eight years of study, I was the most influenced by one of my professors, who taught me 'pattern making'. I think the rest of the students hated him because he was extremely strict. He would make us work on a project for days together. He would take a ruler and measure our work for any difference in measure. He would point out even a 1/8th of an inch of a difference in stitching. He taught us how to stitch a whirl to precision. if it wasn't perfectly straight, if your dart point wasn't done correctly or if it had that tiniest difference, he would pick up his pair of scissors, cut it up and throw it into the bin. That was your entire month's work down the drain. That means you did not put in your final assignment.

So for me, that was an amazing way to learn, until you were perfect at it. I ended up making six blazers, until it came out absolutely perfect, to the point where it could have been some Savile Row, or some really amazing Italian or British tailoring brand. That's the formula we follow till today. My team hates me for it, but we make sure that the quality and the fit is absolutely perfect. if it's not, it's not acceptable.

At what age did you decide to take up Fashion as a profession? Did you parents help you decide? Do you still have second thoughts, sometimes, about your career choice?

Taking up 'Fashion Designing' as a career option was an unconscious decision. I grew up in that atmosphere, it's in my blood. When I started sketching and creating unique articles from scraps of fabric from my dad's shop, Badasaab which was a men's tailoring business. So the kind of fabric scraps that I had, were of course, too plain- very, very men's kind of samples. I would sit with the junior most tailors, so that I was not wasting anyone's time; Seeing something that I had envisioned come to life was extremely fascinating for me. I don't remember being anything else in life, other than a fashion designer. Very unconscious decision, but I knew from the age of maybe four or five, that this is what I was going to be.

People started complementing me on my designs. They would just come up to me asking where I had got a particular design from, so that they could also lay their hands on it. Such incidents gave me the confidence to move ahead.

As far as choosing the wrong profession or the right one, well, I've never had any regrets, whatsoever. I have done my share of hard work - I did an internship with a photographer in Los Angeles, which is quite commendable. So you see I never look back on anything with a sad face. On the contrary I am satisfied with the way my vision has unfolded over the years.

But sometimes I do feel that if I get another chance of reliving my life, I would avoid starting my own company. It gets very tough sometimes, a lot of people have co-founders and partners or other people from the family to support them in the business. It's more of a family affair. Even if you look today at all the successful Indian fashion designers, they all have one person who's handling creative and another who's handling other affairs of the business. As for me, I have done everything singlehandedly.

Someone has truly said that the grass is always greener on the other side. Secretly I now wish that it would have been better if I would have worked with an amazing company, did really well, had that security and that experience, unhindered by the nitty gritty of administration. Handling business affairs sometimes can get really tough because your business mind just kills your creativity. Many a times, months went by before I could get time to put my creativity on paper. Business issues can hinder your inspiration.

Keeping in mind, the kind of training you went through, is there any advice you would like to give to younger women who are starting out, in their careers?

I think it's really important to know your craft, in whatever field you are planning to start. There are a lot of people who think that things can happen ad hoc, especially in fashion, because now people are just pulling pictures from the internet and passing it to a tailor. Little do they realize that it doesn't work that way. I think it's really, really important to know your craft to the minutest of details, more so ever now in this age of the internet, because competition is really tough. Whatever field the person decides to work, the experience and the learning in the actual working field is way more valuable than just theoretical knowledge. So technical knowhow, combined with practical experience would be a foolproof ladder to a successful venture. I also think, for anyone who's starting a business, it's really important to identify a 'need' in the market, because there are too many people doing the same thing. So unless you're really filling a want or a need, don't do it.

How did your brand become a wedding brand?

How my brand started is a long and interesting story. When I came back after completing my studies abroad, I decided to take a loan from my dad, as I wanted to start my label the right way and to put the right processes in place. The ecommerce market was booming internationally. That was the way to go. So, I decided that I was going to start an e-comm brand called Koëcsh, Its specialty being : 'fashion to express yourself'. I started creating a few pieces at a time, at very affordable prices. I decided to name it Koëcsh because I did not want to attack my label, nor to impact the success or failure of my brand.

I started my website, which clicked instantly. I was doing

very, very well. I was invited to take part in Lakme fashion week, which gave me a sponsor, solo show.

But that doesn't mean that I haven't faced any challenges. Someone who hasn't seen failures can never be successful. Somewhere down the line, my software partners became a mess. I had created a custom-made website, paid a lot of money for it, therefore my operating costs were very high. My website crashed even before I had broken even. I not only lost the time and opportunity while it was down, we lost our data too. It was impossible to trace our clients from a crashed website, not to mention the expenses that were piling up. It took us a good, four and a half months to sort that out. We had a long list of dissatisfied clients as they had paid already. It was painful to rebuild from scratch. In fact at this point mine was more like a tailoring shop, because I had to do everything under the sun, to make ends meet.

While I was still in doldrums about creating a new website, I decided to get married. Actually I had been previously engaged, but I had called it off. So these things were simultaneously happening in my life, both career and personal lives were, at an all-time low.

Then I met Vanraj. We decided to get married. That changed everything. For my wedding, my mom took me to visit every place under the sun to find my wedding outfits. The stuff that was available in stores did not appeal to my inner being. Although dresses were beautiful, they simply didn't click with me or my dressing sense. Since, I'm so particular about the quality and the seam, I decided to design my own wedding outfit. Even though I was excited and enthusiastic to begin this new venture, it seemed more of a nightmare for my mom, because Koëcsh was more about self-expression, blacks, tights, studs etc. She was quite fearful that I would end up wearing a black lehenga for the wedding.

I got a bunch of karigars, artisans specializing in their Zardozi and Aari from Pakistan. I learnt the craft and techniques, myself, as I thought it would be an added qualification to my resume. I also learnt embroidery skills. I took the responsibility of dressing up my sister, my husband, my mum, my mum in law, my brother, my dad, and a few of my friends who were traveling, from London and Los Angeles, for the wedding, in addition to creating my own trousseau. Being me, of course every fit had to be different, each outfit had to be creative, and of course, personal to the wearer. So I studied this craft for a long time, while I was in the markets with my Karigars, understanding material and how it is used. It was necessary to do so. After all, a wedding is a special affair.

While designing my wedding lehenga, my sole aim was to make a masterpiece. It had to stand out, as ours was a crazy love story. So I decided to imprint our 'love story' on it. The result was undoubtedly the most novel of an idea put into practice. The entire lehenga, from left to right, had the story unfolding itself. When my dad sat in the mandap he was like - is that a dolphin and a champagne glass on the lehnga? I wore it for my wedding, but didn't reveal the true story behind it, to anyone.

Then we went for our honeymoon. Obviously, I didn't think about work. I said, I'm just going to celebrate 'us', being together and our marriage.

Three months later, when I came back, a lady who writes a blog, and also a friend, told me to write a piece on my unique wedding lehenga. I quickly penned down something and sent it to her. The next morning, when I woke up, I had 800 emails in my inbox all complimenting and appreciating my lehenga. It was not only a dress, but a concept of preserving happy memories and cherishing them for a lifetime. My server had crashed as it was unable to bear so many emails. My Instagram had blown up - I had messages from Korea, Pakistan, the UK and Australia, to name a few. Each one of them wanted a lehenga, unique enough as mine, for their wedding. That is how my new label, my namesake label, was born.

This fame may be playing haywire with life balance. How do you balance your family's expectations vis a vis your work commitments?
When I come home for dinner, my husband is always by my side, supporting me. So that pressure has never been felt. I can easily attribute my achievements in life to my husband who has been extremely understanding, which is not the case with my dad. He has had problems with my pre occupation, at times. There are still some moments, when I'm sitting with my dad and he tells us to put our phones away. "Doesn't matter" he says " work will always be there. What if you're on a flight or on a diving trip? So put your phone away and let's have a drink or let's have a meal."

Being a creative person, do you feel the pressure of your own expectations?
No. I would say it is similar to someone who loves cooking. A cook just feels at ease, once they're in the kitchen and when something 'is cooking'. They enjoy eating it even more. In more ways than one, I have enjoyed my profession, I've had my fair share of it. I traveled a lot when I was studying. I went out to party with friends all night, I came home at four or five in the morning. There was nothing that I didn't do. For a creative person these are the kinds of things that inspire you, travelling, exploring new things, going to a club or just

imagining something out of the box, whether it's to do with music, the environment or the people you meet.

Of course, there were times where we would have to handle an extraordinary project, especially in Parson's New York, where the professors would tell us to churn out like 200 sketches by the next day. I think they were just trying to test our perseverance so that they could classify and ascertain a certain level of class for us. There were times where I wanted the ground to open up and swallow me. But I went with the flow.

Is it true that creative people are affected by their moods?
Sometimes, of course you can't help it. But luckily ever since I've been married, my husband and I we have a pact that we will leave work, back at office. If at all there's something to deal with, we can come back to it the next day. I think it's really important to have a work life balance. However as I'm extremely, extremely passionate, work stops being work and becomes a passion.

Have you ever had to face any gender stereotyping in your work?
Luckily for me, no, never. I have an extremely supportive family. This goes both to my maternal and paternal sides as well. it's been great since the beginning, because I've learnt many lessons from our culture and history. So it's only been positive for me.

What do you think is the best professional dress for women in India?
In the fashion industry, we don't have any major dress codes. My team at the store have been told to wear black, be it dresses,

pants, anything that expresses them and their individuality. But for me personally I don't know if I am the right person to comment, since I have never experienced it.

What would you say to girls with very demanding careers, would you advise them to get married?
I think it depends from person to person. It also has a lot to do with other factors like family support, husband, in laws, your financial situation, city you live in and what you deal with. Different cities have different safety factor for girls. If the person has the opportunity and the support, then I don't see why it would not work.

Do you think that it is necessary to get married to feel fulfilled in life?
No absolutely not. A lot of people have it as a box that they have to check at a certain age. My generation and the next were raised very differently in the internet world. I think women have become much more independent, much more career oriented. To be very honest with you, I don't think we have the tolerance that maybe our mothers or grandmothers' or great grandmothers did. Which is why, the rate of divorce is so much higher today. It's important to get married, if it's something you really want and you genuinely get along with that person. It's really sad that out of all my friends that are married, I can count on my fingers, the ones that are happy in their marriage, with their in-laws and with their situation. It's really sad.

I have a really amazing group of young unmarried girls at work, who receive bio-data of guys for matrimonial purpose. My advice to them is that they should not go ahead with it unless they're sure about it. Their parents probably would not agree with me, but this is who I am.

Tell me something about yourself. What do you find motivating or demotivating? How do you renew yourself?
In terms of what motivates me, it has changed. Earlier, I had a checklist about reaching targets, where I wanted my brand to be. Post COVID, my team became my biggest motivator. I have a team of 100 people, for whom I feel responsible for putting food on their table. My store was shut for four months, there was absolutely no income coming in. The aim now was how to make things happen. Changing the business formula, figuring offline options or virtually anything under the sun, I tried to figure out ways to sustain myself and my staff.

Now, post COVID, the brand is doing amazingly well. But I wouldn't stop here. What is next on my bucket list? I'm working on launching a men's wear brand and a swimwear brand, to be more specific.

What puts you off?
I'm someone with a very short temper, but things like wastage, mess ups at work, when something is done wrong or fabric is used very carelessly. That just gets me really upset.

What, in your opinion, is the common mistake made by working women?
I think women tend to play it safe, hence most of the times they do not follow their passion.

How would you like to be remembered by your peers?
I want to be known for my meticulous work, done with precision. I am like a tiger, unafraid to fight for what I believe in.

In hind sight, is there anything that you would have done differently?
I wish I had studied less and started my career earlier. I feel, being 'on the job' has given me much more practical, first-hand knowledge, than any of the formal course or training. In the end I would like to add that I've always believed in my gut, but it's taken me time to do that.

" My take on Kre'sha Bajaj

Her upbringing

Kre'sha though an entrepreneur like Deena, but her interview is as different as chalk from cheese. That is because unlike Deena, KRE'SHA knew from age five that she wanted to be a fashion designer. To understand what role her environment played, we must remind ourselves that her own parents had also broken the mould. Her father at the age of 16 started a men's apparel business which was very popular with the Indian Film Industry and her mother started the first Benetton store in Mumbai. Her reality is that a) entrepreneurship and fashion trend setting is in the blood. This is their currency. The remarkable thing here is they have been able to nurture KRE'SHA's creativity to cross the frontiers of beauty and business, which happens only in few families. b) There is complete honesty/ integration here, which is a necessary trait to be an artiste. What is in their heart, in the deepest, darkest corner even, they will express in their art. A dishonest person cannot be a good artiste. That honesty integrates the inner self with its outer persona. How well KRE'SHA is integrated, is reflected in her communication, her personal life, and her business.

Her Career

From this integrated person, springs forth a personality woven into her creations. Whether it is her rebelliousness or her curiosity or her experiences as a traveler, her visual world all find expression in her work. She lives through her creation. While the right schools and teachers have developed her technique and helped perfect her process, it has also given her the self-confidence to learn the mastering of new forms / types of work. She holds high standards, a trait for which her work cannot be duplicated. And she is self-driven which bodes well for the growth of her brand. KRE'SHA exemplifies how women can convert their "love" into a thriving business, an approach which is different from adrenaline powered businesses. I find her interview a must read for creative people who would like to monetize their creativity.

Leadership

To that extent her leadership is derived from her real-world experiences. Her drive for perfection and uniqueness, values she has imbibed growing up, her integrity, her days as Activity Prefect. These have made her a risk taker, decisive, hungry for more, goes with her gut and accountable, qualities visible in her style and in this interview.

Women specific

Having been brought up in a very egalitarian household, for KRE'SHA the gender issue will always be the externalities of their environment which is India's reality – the kind of household the girls are brought up in, the city; and her own personal experiences aka her friends' and the young set of girls who work with her. She shares her own observation honestly.

Sushmita Chakravarty
SOCIAL WORKER

THE MOMENT ONE reads Sushmita's interview, one feels that she has given up a lot by giving up her career. But when you talk to her, i.e. if you are lucky enough to find her standing still long enough to answer your call, you will be surprised to find that the lady is busier now than she was during her corporate career. The happiness she is emanating is perhaps from the happiness she is spreading. You are the source, right?

She is busy emceeing events, lending her might to causes she believes in, living what we understand as "A Meaningful Life". I had covered her in my first book as well, "Have the women left Venus? Decoding gender @ workplace" for this very reason. And therefore who better represents there is Life After Work, than Sushmita.

Here is an upshot of her career:
- ❖ NGOs and Social Organisations, April 2014 - Present (8 years 7 months) Consultant
- ❖ Dignity Foundation, June 2017 - October 2019 (2 years 5 months) Chief Dignitarian, Delhi Chapter
- ❖ CSC India October 2005 - March 2014 (8 years 6 months) Associate Director

- ❖ Perot Systems February 2003 - October 2005 (2 years 9 months) Project Director
- ❖ FMSC/Computershare 1997 - 2000 (3 years)
- ❖ Account Manager 1995 - 1997 (2 years) NIIT Technologies Project Manager
- ❖ CMC Ltd 1987 - 1994 (7 years) Systems Engineer

And her educational background:
1. IIT Delhi, M.Sc. Mathematics – (1984-1986)
2. St. Stephen's College, Delhi B.SC, Mathematics - (1981 - 1984)

Turn overleaf for the deep dive into her upbringing to decode the DNA of women pioneers.

Thu, 12/23 10:46AM • 1:01:05

What kind of family environment did you grow up in? Was it a joint or nuclear family?
I was the only child of my parents. My father was a pioneer in the field of Russian language in India. In fact, he was the first Indian to get a scholarship to go to Russia and learn Russian and then establish Russian teaching in India. He later joined Jawaharlal Nehru University. Initially he was in Delhi University, went on to join JNU, held various administrative posts and finally retired from there. My mother was a journalist by profession before her marriage. But when she relocated to Delhi, she didn't join anything immediately, until I was a little older. Then she picked up Spanish and Portuguese and started teaching English to foreign diplomats. She didn't want a nine to five kind of job. This gave her the flexibility. My childhood has been wonderful. I studied in St. Anthony's school. It is in Safdarjung Development Area, just opposite IIT Delhi. And the school started with a few students, eight to 10 students and I was one of them. So of course, school has always been extremely, extremely special to me.

Was it very traditional / conservative?
I would say they were not at all conservative. They wanted to maintain tradition in the sense so they made sure I learn to read and write in Bengali. So, they taught me at home. But

they were never conservative. In fact, when I was working, I got a job offer through NIIT, abroad, in Indonesia. At that time, most of my peers were going to USA. I hadn't the slightest inclination to go abroad. It was they who encouraged me and said, this will enrich you personally and professionally. They pushed me. They encouraged me to take part in extracurricular activities, whether it was in school or college. I anchored events, I'm a voracious reader.

Being the only child, was the environment very strict? Was there any messaging around gender-based stereotypes?
Two things that come to my mind are that other families were very clear that they will send their daughters to a girl's college. My parents had absolutely no such stipulation. Their only objective was that you should get admission into a good college. Many of the families were absolutely horrified because my father was initially in Delhi University, mother also after she married my father. They were in DU (Delhi University) campus, so my father was very keen that whichever good college I get into, I should get exposure to campus life. It was hard though, because travelling from JNU to DU everyday was very taxing. He said it will give you a very good exposure and he was right, it was different from school where we were highly protected. But they did not want to choose a college based on convenience - that it's near home, you won't have to commute much, or, it's a totally girl's college. They were in fact very keen that I go into a Co-ed college, even St. Anthony's was co-education at that time when we started. it's a healthier atmosphere, to go to a Co – ed. Luckily, I had the marks to go to St. Stephen's so that was also good exposure.

Who were you in school, the teacher's pet, the class bully or the book worm? And how did that shape you?
Yes. I was reasonably good at studies. What happened was, in class seven, we had a very dynamic class teacher called Mrs. Rita Ratnam. She was also our vice principal and our English teacher, a wonderful teacher, a wonderful singer, she used to play the piano, and the next moment, you would see her on the basketball field playing basketball equally well. She started pushing me to take part in recitation competition and debate. When she first told me to take part in an Inter House debate, I was a nervous wreck and expressed my reluctance to take part and that too to my mom, who happened to be an All India debating champion. So, my father said, you have a champion at home, you jolly well are going to take part in this.

If it is anybody, other than my parents, who has changed the course of my life, or my personality, it has to be Ratnam ma'am. After that, I started taking part in a lot of inter school competitions and won a lot of medals and Cups. The book worm tag I won't agree to, but yes, I did give a lot of importance to studies and extracurricular activities as well.

Did that trend continue in college also?
To a lesser extent, because IIT is very large and you do have these engineering schools. In Stephen's off and on, IIT less.

Surprisingly, when I went to work, Dr. PP Gupta was a very keen enthusiast of these activities. We used to have Fests every two years, we had Annual days. So, that continued, anchoring the events or taking part in competitions. It continued even later, in CST where I last worked. Even now, I take part in book reading sessions or anchor events. Wherever I get an opportunity, I do it.

Would you say that initial push translated into confidence building and that formed a strong foundation for your career?
Absolutely. Had it not been for that push or encouragement in school, I don't think I would have been able to stand up in front of an audience and debate or compete, recite, or do a declamation.

In CSC, I have anchored three-hour events to an audience comprising 6000 people. I don't think I would have had the confidence to do that had it not been for Mrs. Ratnam's encouragement. I remember a parent teacher meeting where my parents had asked Mrs. Ratnam, that she's taking on so many extra-curricular activities though she's doing extremely well, do you think it'll affect her studies? I recall Ratnam Ma'am saying it will not. You will realize the value of this later, which they knew, but they were just a wee bit worried that we may be giving more importance to that side of the school curriculum rather than the study.

When did you start thinking about who or what you want to become? Is there any incident which was the turning point – which influenced your career choice?
After I graduated, I applied for different exams. I had got through in the MCA (Master's Computer Applications) course in Delhi University and MSC IT; but, having failed the rigorous routine of commuting daily from JNU to DU, I told my parents that it would be much better if I stayed in a hostel in DU while I do this master's course. Unfortunately, the hostels at that time, were giving priority to students from outside Delhi. So, I took the decision of doing MSC from IIT Delhi as I got hostel there. In the second year starting from the 3rd semester, we had a specialization, which could be

pure mathematics or statistics or computer science, so I chose computer science and that's where I got interested.

I completed my post grad in '86. I then started applying for jobs. Fortunately, I got through an IT company called CMC limited, which has now been taken over by TCS and is known as CCS only. That was the start.

The IT industry was in its nascent stage. It wasn't as if it was totally nonexistent, but it was just starting to pick up. And CMC was a well-known name, because when IBM wound up its operations in India, many of their senior people started this company to maintain all the IBM hardware. It started out like that, as Computer Maintenance Corporation. It later became CMC limited when they branched off into software and other things. So when I got an offer, obviously we consulted people. Everybody was very positive about money and the opportunity. So I didn't have any apprehensions and I was keen to join an IT company rather than an IT department in a company from a different industry. I wanted my growth in the IT industry. I was very clear about that.

My father did his bit and spoke to some people in JNU, they all said, just go for it. They had been very, very encouraging.

After eight years in CMC, when I had an opportunity to go abroad, I was keen to go to Indonesia only for two and a half year. After that I said I'm coming back. Then out of the blue, I got an offer from Sydney. I remember calling them from Jakarta. My father said you are crazy about Australia, Go. Just go. So I came back to India, as the visa and stuff had to be done from here. I went abroad on one condition that they will visit me wherever I go. And this is a promise they fulfilled. I'm happy about that. They used to come for 2 to 3 months; we traveled a lot.

Where did you acquire your professional education and training? I understand your father worked in JNU. Did that exposure help you in any way?
A lot on the job actually. Having said that I was heavily influenced by my father because, apart from being a teacher, he also held a lot of administrative positions. I had seen him in action. JNU being a campus, people would drop in at home, it's not like Office finishes at 4 pm. I had the opportunity to observe him. He held the highest position, was Dean of Students, which is number three in the hierarchy. My father was so cool in his approach and thorough in execution.

I saw the leadership in my father then. He was extremely principled. When I went overseas, he said, make it a point to make friends with the people of that country. Believe it or not I'm still in touch with them after 20 years. Be it clients or colleagues, I am still in touch. So yes, I will say parents first and then on the job.

When you are abroad, it's very important to understand the culture of the people you're working with. Specially if you're in a leadership position. I had clients in Turkey and Norway, and they are like North Pole and South Pole. If you do not understand the culture and the way to communicate and deal with local people in the project, it will be a mess. It's very important to understand the culture, which I made an effort to do. That had an impact.

Did it have any influence on your personality or your career opportunities? What will be your advice to young women about to commence their career?
Some training on leadership helped. But at the end of the day, it has to be on the job. If you have somebody, a leader, who is keen to mentor you, then that's good. I have been very

fortunate to have very good mentors, not just a boss, but very good mentors. And I still mentor some of the people who worked with me, they still call me for advice. I think that's very, very important. I had a mentor, who told me, even if you're going out for a team lunch, just remember your behavior is being observed. It's very important to have these mental states. I know a guy in my team, who would be a nervous wreck while giving presentations.

Technically he was brilliant. As soon as you put him in front of five people, out of nervousness he would stammer. He told me that he started observing me and other good presenters to improve his skills. Once he gave a presentation in front of senior customers, which blew me away. He said, its thanks to the people I observed. These are important ways. First recognize that yes, this is where I have a limitation; two, observe your mentors, don't be afraid to seek help.

It is that willingness to. I remember an instance where it was escalated to me. On an important call with the customer, the girl handling the customer she told her boss (who was reporting to me) that she can't make it for this call. It was critical that she attend because she was handling that part of the project. I suggested to her that she should take the call from home. She agreed. I asked her to suggest this alternative to her boss. The whole scenario changed.

Her project manager had a negative impression that women don't want to stay late, women don't want to do this or that. Some of these issues can be resolved by conversing, finding a middle ground. I'm not saying everything can be resolved easily, this was a simple example. But try to find a solution wherein we can at least try to resolve the issue at hand.

I also see that there is a little bit of a reluctance to network.

That's where women fall behind. There's no easy solution. I would say it's not a crime if women were to keep an eye out for things like this-a little bit of casual meeting does not prevent you from doing your work.

Did the India culture ever prove to be a hindrance to you? How did you handle that?
My bosses abroad were not Indian. The one in Indonesia was a Singaporean. The one in Sydney and London, they were both from Australia. I've never had Indian bosses abroad.

As for cultural no-no's, I've observed among people in my team that when there are two or more Indians in a group, while the rest happen to be from a different country, the Indians start talking in Hindi. That's just not polite, according to me.

Another incident - I was at a customer location for a longish stint of about two months in USA, Rhode Island. A lady from client side came up to me and asked if she could give me feedback? I said, yes of course. She asked me why do "our" people always go out in groups. The correct thing to do is, if you want to go and get a cup of coffee, go down, pick up your coffee from Starbucks come back and have it; or if you want a break, sit there and have it. Indians, however when they go, all will go together to have coffee, or lunch, or smoke, whatever.

That was a learning even for me, that we have to undo some of these habits. So I had a chat with the team and told them that once in a while it's okay for 2 people going out for coffee, but don't make it very obvious. Six people leaving their desk together – a big NO.

I called the whole team, so it doesn't become obvious that I'm pointing out a few people. I just told them a few things about, the culture; that these things you must understand.

Every country has some customs, which we have to adhere to. After all we too expect the same when they come to our country. When we are at a client location, especially when working out of a client location, it's all the more important that our behavior is exemplary. We don't give people a chance to say such things. I gave them a couple of examples. These things are not told to them. They learn by trial and error.

This cross-cultural understanding is very important to be given.

What was it that you struggled with in the initial years? How did you handle that struggle?
Yes, I did. So the turning point came when I went to Indonesia. I went through NIIT and was assigned to a project with Hewlett Packard. I went from a team lead role to a project manager role and the project was to automate two stock exchanges. From a manual system to a completely automated system. I was replacing a guy who had some 20 years more experience than me. So that was the benchmark. Absolutely upfront I'm telling you, I struggled big time. Because understanding everything, then a totally different country. It was very, very tough in the beginning. But I said, no, I'm just not going to give up. I made it a point to understand everything and the technicalities, the intricacies. I still remember one incident.

This is when we had settled down and had automated everything. We were installing phase two of this automation, three days later the system went down. I was called to the stock exchange where the President, the Vice President, and the board of directors, all were there. I still remember the statement of the director saying, madam, you realize Time is money. I got goose bumps. I tried to look calm. I said, yes, but you must also realize that it's an automated system and automated systems can go down, we will work overnight if necessary. We fixed the problem by the evening. For the first time in history, the trading hours were extended. Experience gave me confidence. I made an effort to know the clients, learn the language. I used to speak fluent Indonesian. I think the biggest compliment was when my clients themselves offered me a job when I was leaving Indonesia, saying that we would love to have you with us. But by that time, I already had an offer from Australia, I said, no it's not fair as I've accepted that. I said no, it wouldn't be professional. I said I will always keep in touch, which I do. I think after that, I don't recall any major struggle as such. Challenges yes, that will always happen. That phase is what I call toughest phase in my entire career.

When you look at the management of the job, when you are leading a team of people from different countries it was something within me. A lot of it came from my parents' encouragement, saying you can do it. Plus the inner voice saying don't give up. That for me was the last resort. Self- talk helped.

What about marriage and career? Can marriage gel with career or does a woman have to choose between the two?
Many people think that I chose career over marriage, which is actually not true, I was quite open to marriage. But something just didn't click, to be very blunt and open. My parents were very clear. The proposals that were coming had weird conditions like she has to leave her job. So my father said thank you very much you can leave. It just didn't click. It was not as if I chose to be a career woman. In my mind, I did extremely well in my career and got a lot of opportunities at the right time.

I think both can gel. But what happens is, if you see there

are fewer women at the top because of responsibilities at home. I know women who are extremely good, but they have been telling me that I'm satisfied as a project manager level, I don't want to go to a senior project manager, because I can't give so much time to Office, whether it's from home or whether it's working from home; Even when we were flexible about some hours working from home. Again, it is part of that of Indianness you referred to, there are families where the in-laws are very supportive. The household work is shared. Things are changing. But again, the primary responsibility becomes that of the woman, whether it's managing the house, especially when the kids come that becomes a challenge. I have lost so many excellent ladies in my team, and other teams also. We extended maternity leave, we gave them part time working options, but it didn't work out. They used to feel guilty about leaving this small baby even if it was with their mother-in-law. It is a challenge; I don't have any solution or answer to this.

Yes, they can gel; but how far you rise depends on a lot of other things as well.

Does marriage have anything to do with feeling fulfilled in life?

I find you do miss the companionship. Fortunately, I have a very large circle of friends and a support system. I think about it. But then I also think that had one of those proposals clicked, would I have had such a good career? Would I have gone abroad; would I have had that enrichment opportunity both professionally and personally? Maybe not. so it's a mixed bag. But what I tried to do is keep on being busy with these various activities. So that one doesn't think about it but yes, at some point you think but then honestly, I've seen a lot of, even within my very close friends, some very bitter marriages which have ended in divorces, which has left long lasting impression, terrible scars on these people. They tell me you are better off. It's a mixed thing. I would love to have a companion.

My parents passed away in 2013 and 2014. My parents have had a fantastic marriage so that's my benchmark. it'd be nice to have a companion. That's what I sometimes miss.

Tell me something about you as a person, what you find motivating? What makes you angry? What inspired you to write?

What makes me angry is the easy one - disrespect and lies. I just cannot tolerate disrespect, and I cannot tolerate lies. I have a temper, so I work on trying to remain calm. But earlier on I would be furious at these things.

What motivates me, at some point one also must be self-motivated. I get the opposite, like I remember about a year and a half back, I came across a very famous band in Kolkata called Bhumi. One of their members, Soumitra Rai. He wrote a book called Mr. Adivasi, which is an excellent book. So they did a huge event here.

The publisher told me that they would like me to moderate the whole event, which included reading of the book passages, interviewing the author, handling the Q & A and everything. At the end of the event, when the publisher, who's the founder of the company, hugged me and said, brilliant job, that's huge motivation. So appreciation is obviously a very good motivation. During lock down, I didn't want to be in the doldrums. I can't go out, I'm missing my friends, I think one has to find interests within oneself. So, I started writing points.

I had also started learning music after my corporate career got over, we started virtual events during the pandemic. In this one year, I must have sung some 100 songs. Twice a month we used to meet online, somebody reciting something, it's not all songs. That kept me motivated. And of course walking within the house compound and yoga and this and that. You've got to find things to do. That's the biggest motivation.

What about your peers? How would you like to be remembered by your peers?
I've always had good peer relations, even in office, because one thing I never did was to compare myself with others. I learned to accept that because comparison makes you insecure, which can ruin a lot of options, if you allow insecurity to eat you up, you will lose opportunities you deserve.

People marvel at my network. I would like to be remembered as somebody who's very caring and loving and willing to help others. I think that is very important. That willingness to help is something which has been imbibed in me by my family, especially my parents and people around me, even role models like Dr. Kiran Bedi. I'm the birthday remember-er of the group, the first one to wish. I tell them, guys, please remember mine. I mean I cannot wish myself.

I have interacted with diverse people in my social activities. I've met differently abled youngsters who are excellent painters. And when one of them gave me his painting, I could not stop my tears. We started encouraging him in our company, he got a lot of orders from HCL and others. We gave him an identity; he's earning 50,000 a year now. These things inspire me to keep doing them.

In this whole journey, have there ever been times when you said, maybe I should have done something else? Or handled a particular situation differently?
No. Nothing.

Somebody asked my father, why did she come back after seven years abroad? It was unheard of. I had no intention of settling abroad. Again, no offense meant, I was very clear six, seven years and my father said that she has a to-do list apart from work. Visit Wimbledon etc., etc. All that is ticked off. I still have some things on the to-do list. Mainly travel related. Some unfulfilled, some places that I didn't visit. But I don't think I would have changed anything at all.

In one of the WhatsApp chats I reacted to somebody who happens to be one of my best friends and he took it very badly and he didn't talk to me for two years. We revived our friendship eventually, but it was a valuable lesson. That when you're face to face, you can see the body language, you can see the expression. When you're writing something, stop and think. Don't be impulsive and just react without rhyme or reason. It was a lesson which I've learned specifically related to social media.

There's a quote that the true profession of a man is a way to find himself. So, in your case, what do you think that you have found about yourself in this profession?
So I had a career in IT for 28 years. Since 2014 I have been involved with various NGOs, the dominant one being Dr. Kiran Bedi's NGO, Navjyoti India Foundation, and I'm now on their board as well. In April 2014, I got sick of corporate life and decided to switch to social work completely.

What I have found about myself is that I have the capacity to help others, especially people who are, I will use the word with Dr. Kiran Bedi uses "the underserved". She used a beautiful quote she said we should never call ourselves underprivileged we should call them underserved and it is our privilege to serve them. And I have also found out that it's not about money. Yes, money's important, but sometimes I go to a senior citizens house here, children abroad and auntie all alone, 85 years of age, I just spend time. Leave the pandemic time aside, that was a totally exceptional situation, but just chat for a while or I tell her do you want a book from the library or something like that, she was a good friend of my parents. That joy in her eyes brings an acute smile to my face. Those are things that I am proud about myself, that one should make some time for these things; one should also make time for own self. It is perfectly okay to be at home with a cup of coffee and a good book and listen to music or sing.

Since India opened some 3 decades ago, do you think the attitude of people working together, both men and women, have changed for the better?
If I look back at my 25-to-30-year career maybe some improvement but I wouldn't say that huge change has happened; like I mentioned earlier, some changes do happen like for example, I had a project manager and he realized he's got 20 people in his group and all men. So I called him and I said why haven't you taken any girls in the team? And he said, no, same response - they have to stay late, they can't do this, they can't do that, we need people who can work and blah blah blah I said you please try. Then at the end of 1.5 years he had 60% women in his team. He said that is the greatest piece of advice you gave me.

So I would say yes, mentality has changed. I have never faced, honestly, either here or abroad, this gender problem. So, personally it's been fine for me. There were 1 or 2 people who would have a little trouble with a woman boss, maybe its upbringing, maybe it's the background they come from, I don't know and I don't want to be judgmental. But looking at the larger picture there were very, very few.

"My take on Sushmita Chakraborty

Upbringing

Sushmita is Destiny's Child. She had the perfect parenting, perfect teacher and parent-teacher alignment which resulted in her confidence in a) exploring a new field i.e. Computers for her first career, and b) Emceeing as a second career post-retirement. "Had it not been for that push or encouragement in school……" many of us wouldn't have a rich fulfilling life post 50's.

The unique thing about her upbringing was her learning about other cultures that she imbibed from a role model father and mother.

Career

I admire Sushmita for the composure with which she has conducted her career and assertive way she has handled her bosses. Nobody taught her that, she must have seen the same things we all had, like respect your elders, don't talk back etc. all the normative sentences. Despite that she has been able to handle all the interculturally sensitive situations. It is this competency which has got her assignments abroad, people watching her conduct herself with elan and opening up international career. It is a testimony to her capability that she has never had to look for work while work has found her.

I also admire her for walking out of the corporate sector without any regrets and taking up her hobby, Emceeing. as a 2nd career. Hobbies make us well rounded and help us form a healthy self-image.

Leadership

When asked about India culture, Sushmita has not touched upon Patriarchy which means it is not in her frame of reference. For her the world is equal, making her an Inclusive leader. I think she is a rare quality, the desire to spend her sunlight years serving the "underserved", creating emotional and social capital, authentically.

Women Specific

For youngsters, she has a very important tip to give, that "try to find a solution wherein you try to resolve the issue at hand". That's how you navigate your career. For women who manage people I am going to use this opportunity to say that don't despair if your parents have not travelled abroad. Do read books written by women authors of other countries or watch their webinars. You will learn about other countries and will gain confidence in displaying your womanly qualities, how to integrate your softer abilities with your hard ones.

And remember when your perspective changes, so will your outer reality.

Kanika Saxena
MSDT, VP MARKETING VODAFONE

YOU WILL FIND a difference here. When you read Kanika's resume, it reads like a high achiever's. But then it takes an interesting turn. So, I am not sure which one will be more meaningful for you – her first career or the second one? The first career proves that if you work hard, put your nose to the grind, be one up on your colleagues, you will realize your dreams. She made the right moves, gained the trust of her bosses, and learnt the art of navigating her career. And yet she gave it all up to become a Scuba Diving Trainer. What was it in her career that was so dissatisfying? Makes us question our own borrowed versions of "career".

Well, read her story here. But first a look at her thumbnail sketch:

- 2018 onwards Vice President Digital Content Services with Vodafone Idea Limited (Vi)
- 2017 – 2018: Business Head – Trigger Happy Entertainment Network (THEN), led the Business Development, Content Production & Entertainment Marketing mandate.
- 2015 – 2018: Founded Why? Stay! Calm! Entertainment a Branded Content agency. Led creation for 45 blockbuster

films in India. Eventually merged with THEN in 2017. Shot and trained top Bollywood stars for underwater sequences for films including titles like Amazon Obijjan, Rangoon, Dishoom, Kalakandi & Ananya Birla's music album.
- 2012: Infused capital and launched a 32-seater specialty Bengali restaurant "Bong".
- 2010 – 2014: Marketing Strategist- (Fox Star Studios, Balaji Motion Pictures and Dneg): Collaborated with international entities across Toronto, London, and the US and brought postproduction projects to India, including Sin city 2, Gravity, Maleficent, Total Recall & The amazing Spiderman
- 2009 –2010: Head Marketing - UTV Bindass: Took channel GRP from 14 to 41
- 2007: Sony Pictures Network, Marketing Manager, launched & managed promotion of 9 primetime, high viewership shows - Indian Idol season 2&3, Big Boss-1, Jhalak Dikhla Ja-1.
- 2005: Senior Research Manager - Zee Entertainment set the premise for brand basis research, competitive scenarios, insights & market intelligence.
- 2002: Worked with global media agencies like Group M(Mindshare/Motivator), developed sales pitches winning clients for the agency & designed media plans.

She has had a stint as an entrepreneur as well, which is not unexpected as quite a few women end up doing, a point elaborately discussed in my first book "Have the women left Venus? Decoding gender @ workplace". Her dive (pun intended) into a scuba diving career with its peculiar struggles and personal angst "unseen" on a resume. This is the triumph of the human spirit, a state of mind which does not exist in an employer's lexicon. Ultimately, what we need to remember is that we live our life for ourselves, not for others.

Educational Qualifications:
- 2013 - Master Scuba Diver Trainer (MSDT) - Professional Association of Diving Instructors, Koh Tao, Thailand
- 2002 - PGDM in Marketing | ITM Business School, Bombay, India
- 1993 - Bachelor of Business Management |Administrative Management College, Bangalore, India.

A string of recognitions followed:
1. Recipient of India Top 100 Women Icon by India Prime Awards (2021)
2. Recipient of Excellence Award in recognition for outstanding professional achievement & contribution in Nation building by Indian Achievers Forum (2020)
3. Recognized as one of Top 50 Most Influential marketing professionals in World Marketing Forum (2018) India's second female Master Scuba diver trainer & Instructor certified by PADI with 7 specialties in deep-sea diving instruction.

I call her a one-woman portal. Kanika has learnt the hard way, she has experienced the struggles a woman can go through, and still rise above it, to have her name written for posterity, as:

India's 2nd Woman Master Scuba Diving Trainer

Now read her story:

Interview Tue, 3/15 12:41PM • 23:40

What kind of family environment did you grow up in? Was it a joint or a nuclear family?
Well we were a mixed bag. My father's side were all government servants. He grew up in a joint family. My mom's family, on the other hand, were all professionals. But ours was a nuclear family. There were four of us. So, there were all these conflicting influences when I was growing up.

Can you describe this influence?
My father's family was a joint family, hailing from Banaras. He moved to Lucknow when I was born. He was working in The Geological Survey of India as a scientist. His elder brother never got married and was the head of the family. He called the shots for all the brothers and their families. My grandfather from my mother's side, was a doctor, a self-made man. All her family members were well educated. Although both families were well educated, it was my mother's side which was more progressive.

Lucknow is the city I have grown up in during the formative years of my childhood. Because my father was very attached to Banaras, very frequently we would travel to Banaras. There we had to play by the rules of the family. We had to be dressed more conservatively. The women of the house were frowned upon if they showed skin. Wearing jeans was a no-no, all my other cousins who lived there were always in a salwar kurta and a dupatta. Raising your voice was frowned upon.

Thanks to my dad though, those diktats never applied to me. On my mum's side, my aunts were educated, everybody had the freedom to express their opinion. She believed you must be dressed in accordance with fashion, wear short clothes, wear everything, be more open. So that's how I grew up.

But finally, we have to remember that freedom has a shelf life. Even if the girls got educated, became a doctor, engineer or whatever but finally the family will find a boy from the same caste and get the girl married.

From both sides of the family, by these standards, I am a black sheep.

What were some of stories you were fed to justify the environment at home. Any incidents which had a lasting impact on self-confidence?

I have a younger sister who was born physically disabled. My parents were busy taking her for surgeries to different parts of the country since she was two years old. I was eight years old at that point of time. For most of my childhood I ended up being self-reliant.

My father would try to leave me in Lucknow, but I preferred to live in my own house. I had a dog, who was my only companion. Daily, I would go to my grandmom's house in Lucknow in a public transport bus, deposit the dog there, go to school, go eat at her place, come back home, lock both the doors of my house. There was a servant in the house who used to live there. Emotionally I learnt how to deal with any situation.

There were many restrictions regarding dress, but my dad never forced it on me. However, it made me question why the women of the house cannot have a voice. It's an ecosystem you grow up in, where all your aunts and cousins do not have a word; including the boys actually, but I always saw my mom having a word. My mom was the odd person out, so to speak, among the women in the family because she had a point of view. I was witness to her displeasure with whatever was going on in that household. That changed me. I ended up having a voice too, questioning my dad over whatever was being done to me or to the women around me. It was not something that was taught to me. It was what I became as an outcome of what I saw. As a girl child when you live by yourself in a city like Lucknow which was not that modern, it is hard, but I learnt to rely on myself.

I don't think anybody should be told what they should do. We should have the freedom to make our own lives, the way we want to.

My refuge those days were books. I was a hardcore reader. My education happened primarily through the medium of reading. I would go to my mum's school, sit in the library, get all 20 books from the likes of an Enid Blyton to Richie Rich, Mills & Boon, Agatha Christie, Hardy Boys etc. I would come home, plant myself on the bed, forget eating, sleeping; just disappear into my books. Reading became my outlet, it helped understand what was happening outside Lucknow.

So, for me it was books, or friends, whoever gave me love and affection. I was very guarded and vulnerable as a child. I had to become self-reliant at a very early age and that has defined the rest of my life's journey.

What about school? Were you the studious type, the active sportswoman or the backbencher? How did that shape you?

I was not studious at all. I was an absolute rebel. Till class eight or nine my mom, who was by the way a teacher, used to teach us. From class nine, I went for tuitions. She had very high expectations from me, I had to come 1st in class. I was okay, not very great. I was a backbencher, more of a tomboy, rebellious most of the time.

Till class six I went to a Co-ed school, Cathedral School, which was one of the very good schools of Lucknow. I would beat up the boys and they would not beat me back because they had been taught not to hit girls. Even on my birthdays, all boys would be invited. I had no girlfriends. Then my parents moved me to a girl's school, called Carmel Convent. My mother thought that will subdue me; Instead, I became rebellious, not scared of anybody. Unlike the other girls who by this time are gearing up to adopt their roles in life, my ambition was that this is not what my life should be.

At the age of 14, I used to play basketball, learn music, play the guitar. That was my way of expressing myself.

When did you start thinking about who or what you want to become? Is there any particular incident which was the turning point – which influenced your career choice?
I did not know what I wanted to become. In school I wanted to be an engineer or a pilot. I gave my engineering entrance exams but I did not get the right grades to get in and I didn't want to go to a polytechnic. My parents wanted me to be a doctor, but I did not want to be one. I used to faint at the sight of an infection, which made me unfit to be a doctor.

I remember when I went for 12th admission. I took the money from my father, lied that I had joined biology group (PCB) but actually joined Maths group (PCM). I went through one quarter session in Maths, without my parents coming to know. Finally, my Ma came to know.

After my 12th I wanted to get away from Lucknow and

prove that I can be somebody but didn't know how. I felt horrible in that restricted life. At that point in my life, the only thing I knew was I don't want to live here. My mom's friend was there, she was like a friend to me too, she would always keep an eye on me. She told me about business management. It sounded interesting, so I decided to do business management. Off I went to do my business management. We went to Delhi, didn't like the school there, finally found one in Bangalore.

That's when I started living alone. My father used to travel down from Lucknow to Bangalore.

In the 90's travelling was not what it is like today, that you could hop onto a plane and reach in no time. One had to change many flights. He explained to me that he can't be like other parents and come and pick me up when things get tough, just to test me. I did hunger strike for two months, lived on watermelon to get my parents to agree. Finally, my father relented. My father always had a soft corner for me. He was determined that he would educate me. My mom's best friend came home, helped me pack my bags, label my clothes, gave me tips what to do in a hostel. I joined my parents and sister in Vellore. From there the entourage came to Bangalore to drop me.

I remember standing in the hostel. A feeling of euphoria came over that I'm finally alone, which quickly changed to a feeling of dismay that Oh My God I am alone. It was a tough moment in my life.

So that's how my story began in Bangalore.

There was no looking back after that. I went to do MBA in Mumbai. There I watched a lot of television. That's when I knew that I wanted to work in television. How I am going to do it, what work and how, I was not clear. I was great at writing. I was a great storyteller.

That is all I knew.

What did you struggle with in the initial years?
I remember falling sick in the first month of my BBM and ending up in a hospital. That time I realized I am resilient. When you're home you are surrounded with people, doing whatever you are, even if you're not with family, you feel their presence. But here there was nobody now, but still I managed. One day I got an appendicitis pain. I was rushed to a hospital by one of my roommates. She was a very big influence in my life, a timid Kashmiri girl doing her MBA. I took care of myself. I went through the operation, did everything, I had hundred boys from my class standing outside the door. There were people helping me, Lumina, my friend pawned her gold bangles to pay the hospital deposit till my father arranged money and sent it through a friend, to pay for the surgery. I knew that now that I am out, I am not going back without achieving something.

During semester breaks, while other students went home, I would take a project so that I could learn. I worked with CB Richard Ellis for free which is one of the largest real estate companies, during one of the breaks, just to get experience. Or I would go with my friend to her home. I just wanted to educate myself, learn. I knew that I will have to make many sacrifices, if I wanted to change my life. I would study, go to college, that's it. I was thin and scrawny at that point.

Because I needed more money, so I started modelling. I never asked my father for more money than what he had already provided for - my hostel fees and education. Whatever I needed, I earned it by myself. I remember my first-time waiting tables at Pizza Hut and getting Rs 800 salary for it. Out of that also, the company deducted Rs 550 for uniform, the first time. However small, I was determined I will earn my own living, I'm going to be self-dependent. That was the beginning.

Thanks to those holiday jobs, I realized there was no job which was menial. Everything is equal, because as long as you're earning, every experience counts. Between my modelling assignments and Pizza Hut, I finished my 3 years of BBM. I even got an opportunity to go for an exchange program, as a model.

At this point I was seeing somebody from Bangalore. He came from a very rich, conservative family. However, it did not last long as he did not have the balls to stand up for us. I decided to leave Bangalore, joined ITM in Mumbai to do my MBA. The college had more men than women. I was breaking stereotypes even then because I was clear and vocal, therefore not very popular with the boys. Only some of the women were serious about getting a degree.

Where did you acquire your professional education and training? What was your thinking process when you got your first company in the placement season at ITM?
As a matter of fact, I didn't get placed through ITM. Media was not something the college offered, and because I was already interning in a media company, they said others needed the opportunity. Fortunately, I was picked up by an agency named Group M. I was there from 2002 to 2005.

To me Media was first. I worked with Meenakshi Menon for two years of my life. Then I met Chanda who was one of the buying heads. She had a don't-mess-with-me attitude, sharp as a knife, very affirmative, knew exactly what she wanted. Meenakshi is also like that. So, these were two women I watched day in and day out. Carat was mostly women –

strong, powerful, supportive women who never hesitated in calling a spade a spade. That's how I was trained. I had Meenakshi who was very intimidating. I always wanted to be like her. I found a godmother in Chanda who was also my first boss, incidentally. She was the one who shaped my career. To this point I remember how she would teach me to sit on a table, how to drink fine wine, explain what's the difference between wine and whisky, what I should read, how to talk, how to dress. Every Saturday after-office she would meet me at the Hilton coffee shop, between 2 to 4 in the evening in a class conducted by her. She would ask me what did you read over the weekend? I was supposed to tell what I had read and what I had understood. Two to four was bajaaoing (scolding) time. I ended up crying every time. Four to five she was lathering me with affection which was followed by shopping sponsored by her. I was a trainee and even though she was the head of the business, and inaccessible to most, I was the one who was the center of her affection. She took me under her wing and trained me. So during the week if she saw me whiling away my time during lunch she would turn back and say, "Kanika there are two kinds of people in the world. The ones under the iceberg form 95% of the population. 5% are the ones who are over the iceberg. Which would you like to be? There are people who travel by train in Mumbai every day. I have nothing against them, do you want to be one of them or do you want to be on top, you decide". I was not allowed to drink; I was not allowed to smoke or see boys. Nothing. It was just work all the way to become sharper than a needle and sharper than your peers.

I did well there. From Carat, I moved to another bigger media agency, then television and films.

You have not needed anybody or anything else to grow careerwise?
Actually, that is not right. But in terms of my career counselling, Chanda had a major role in shaping me. My friend Sumona, who is like my sister, we are inseparable. So, these two women, I owe them a lot, most of my life in fact. I am what I am today because of them.

In your opinion what are the most common mistakes made by women in the workplace? Going through your own struggle, what would you say to women who are wanting to start their career?
Lot of women come from extreme surroundings, they are beaten, don't have a voice in a conservative family. They are trying to please everybody to avoid being ostracized.

I think what women mostly do is that they don't speak up. For e.g. married women need to go home, but the boss when he turns up, mocks her because she has to go home. But the woman will not open her mouth, that I have finished my work. The boss will see that guys are hanging around. What he doesn't know is that the guys were wasting their time whole day, while the woman was working all day. Or that one girl is smoking or going for a drink with other male colleagues and another is not, so the latter one is not a networker. These are subconscious biases. Women can say, you know what, I get to go home now because this is what I've done and this is what I bring to the table, we'll take it up tomorrow. They are constantly in this rigmarole of pleasing, pleasing, pleasing.

Nature has made women more nurturing, more caring; they want everybody to be together in a decision because that's how we are constructed in an Indian household. Our nature sabotages us.

Also, one thing you must remember – it is your life; you should be in the driving seat and do whatever it takes. If YOU do not stand up for what you want, nobody else will. Man or woman, irrespective. There might be challenges, there might be reasons due to which you're not able to support yourself or you don't have financial help or physical help or whatever. But I believe if you know what you want, and you take that first step, you will always find your way.

Women have always been hindered by their relationships - either brother, sister, cousin, husband, mother-in-law. They disempower themselves, lose their ability to function as individuals.

I don't take away for a minute from my parents and their love and affection for me. I would not have become what I am today, if I had not taken care of myself first. A lot of success and all that I've achieved in my life is because of strangers. People who didn't know me went out of their way to shower love, affection, support, comfort, financial health, physical health, whatever it would take. God just unfolded them in my life. I have no explanation to give. I always had people in my life who were standing rock solid and were saying go live your life. But if I was too timid and scared and didn't do anything, I'll be where I was. You have to be assertive.

Assertion comes with two things. There is passive assertion and there is aggressive assertion. You have to balance both and keep putting across the point that it's a professional horizon. If it means having uncomfortable conversations, then do that even if it's difficult. To have these conversations with men, old men. I've had older men, who've been in the system long, look upon women in a deprecating manner.

But women are peacemakers. that's the feminine nature and energy. We are very good at sensing a situation, but we have to balance things in the right way, without diminishing ourselves. You have to be a man and a woman, both. I don't have to talk like a man to abuse, but still, I can make my point. I don't have to hang in with the boy gang to be respected. If you want respect, then say whatever needs to be said. That's how men are, right? Somebody will say yaar f**k off, I don't agree with you.

Women should stop playing the victim card. Let your work speak for you. I know so many women like that. I have forgotten how a man behaves or a woman behaves. I am aggressive and couldn't care less about other people's opinion but I'm also emotional and I will never hurt people. You have to know when to use what.

When did your leadership journey start and from whom did you imbibe your early leadership lessons? Did the India culture ever prove to be a hindrance to you?
I am one of the only women with my portfolio in the entire organization. Why? because I cannot be judged by other people's perception. I bring to the table what others can't. To reach that place, I always knew I had to do two things – one was having my finger on the pulse of what is happening next; two, have the strength and the perseverance to pursue it. Since I did not come from that great a college, I worked jolly hard to make up for it, find out, empower myself with knowledge. If I was sitting with my peers, I would always have an opinion and more to say.

I still remember when I went for a presentation to one of my clients which was known as Wonder Masala. I was making that presentation. I was a trainee. I'm doing research and making the presentation. Chanda turns around and says "Kanika if you call me at night, I'll f** you, if the presentation is not ready tomorrow I will f**k you.

So, imagine I'm a trainee who has just come out of college, my teeth are chattering with nervousness. I am sitting in the presentation with Meenakshi and her, and she says I know nothing about cooking and masalas, Kanika is great, she'll present. I can't explain to you what I went through, but that was the day I could see my life where nobody else gets the chance, whereas I had these two women who gave me the chance. I won the account as it was a pitch presentation. I choke under the feeling of how much of a role these two women have played in my life, but I did pretty well.

That was the first instance.

In Zee it was all hands and legs kind of work where I got my bearings in Media. Then I went to Sony Entertainment Television. I was part of the team which launched Non-fiction in India. Non-fiction means formatted shows, reality shows. Very first concepts I worked on were Jhalak Dikhla jaa, Indian idol, Bigg Boss, Duss ka Dum. I took on more responsibility. I've always been a workaholic.

I always made it a point to sit in all meetings, came prepared with ideas which I would always give. Most often one of them would be picked up. I was always there for my bosses, not to my peers, but to my bosses, I would be one up. I would go with a presentation, was always prepared. I was never intimidated or subdued, or made excuses that I am "just a trainee" or "It's not my place". That's where I got noticed. That's how I built myself up.

My knowledge expanded from just doing marketing plain Jane to handling stars, handing celebrities in Sony, to working on promo strategy. My portfolio increased because people saw my willingness to do the things, complete the job.

I have two strengths - I'm able to put two and two together.

I'm also a great storyteller. And if I required counsel, I would go back to my godmother (Chanda) and say this is what I have, this is the idea, what do you think I should do? How do I present myself? How do I start? How do I stand out?

I handle very large teams. Over the years I learnt to handle them with compassion and humility.

How do you put across a viewpoint which you know is conflicting with that of a male dominated group?
I work for a telecom company, which has more men than women on top. It can get lonely there. Most women face this problem in most of the specially sectors like banks / telecom etc. Is there a boy's club? Yes. Do women have to get into it? No. So how do you get accepted as equal? Through your work, by being smarter than others, by being one up. I too have had my share of struggles. But I learnt to state clearly what I want. People heard me, Because I spoke from a place of clarity, that this is my path and this is the way I operate.

There are times when I practice tact, there are times when I do not stop. I've learnt to choose my battles carefully. I don't fight smaller battles of ego. I fight larger battles in terms of strategy and where I want to be. I have learnt how to enunciate and to ensure that my boss looks great. Typically, before a discussion I will always text my boss saying, I think this is what it should be, by the way, this one was doing this. I've always ensured that I know two points more than people on the table, especially in my subject matter. If you have anything else in mind, I'm happy to listen. I play that card as well. By the way, this is what should be, by the way, this is what is happening. So, they always kind of have an insight on each other. Knowledge is power.

My professional colleagues are now friends, for years, I

crossed that line between colleagues and friends long time back. Some of them have become friends, confidants, we do trips together etc. So, I use a combination of all those layers. I fight my battles the same way.

I have never stayed in a job because I have to pay the bills and have to tolerate nonsense. I am very clear if you don't stand up for what you want, or what you are, you're not doing justice to yourself.

From Media to scuba diving is a shift which is difficult to comprehend. How did that happen?

Between 2014 to 2016, was an interesting period. In 2014 I restarted my life. Diving was a game changer because a) I was a woman b) I was 35 by then. Everybody else worth their name then in diving was half my age, 18 / 20 – 22.

I decided I want to learn to dive, I want to learn to teach. At this point I met a gentleman named Anees Adenwala who runs the biggest dive school, Orca Dive Club. He helped me understand the new world of deep-sea diving I was getting into. I started training with Anees. I did course after course. One day he said, why don't you come shoot with us. That's how I started shooting underwater for films with them. I worked as a trainer getting paid, it became a second career.

I can say now that I have two loves of my life - one is diving, the other is traveling. It has opened up my mind. I have travelled 51 countries. I have friends all across the globe. It allows me to learn and unlearn every five years something new, which takes you out of your comfort zone. I make time for learning new skills, new things, because I'm very, very clear that if you want to be on top of the game, before you are the best, you ought to be good. Every organization I've worked with, at that point of time, I made a choice that this was something which was going to have a deep impact in my life. It was giving me strength, and a depth of character.

Every time I go into the ocean, I feel I'm so small. We are human beings; we are arrogant in thought. We believe that we are everything in the world and better. Every time I stand in the water, I feel small and the ocean's depth makes me bigger. Depth gives me calmness, gratitude. It allows me to accept that life has been tough. But I have enough and more. If I don't have one part of my life, which might be love, in the parlance of a man or woman. I have abundance of love from people across in my life. I kid you not, every time I've had tears or I've had a tough time physically, financially, emotionally I've always had, not one, but many people. My birthday is a celebration like it's a national holiday.

What about in your professional life? What did you struggle with there?
Kind of little bit yes; because I am not somebody who cannot be told what to do. I am eccentric. I am not somebody who likes people micromanaging me. I work on clarity that this is where we want to go. Everybody agrees on those terms. When you do whatever it takes to go there, how you do it, what you do, then you have to leave me alone, you cannot tell me what to do what not to do, that doesn't bode well with me. Multiple times in my life across my career I've had bosses who just let me be like, do what the hell you want, as long as you deliver, I really don't care as long as you don't murder someone. Then I've had bosses who really want to know everything, etc. but over time, with tact and diplomacy, I've been able to tell them that, hey, let's draw a line. We look at things from a perspective week on week, I'm just giving you an idea of where I'm coming from, week on week, we monitor progress, then

we go align or realign ourselves. That's one.

Two is that at times there is dissonance etcetera. At that point in time, I choose. I am very clear that every outfit I've been part of, if I don't agree to the concept, I don't work. I've never worked in my life for money, let me reiterate this. I work for passion; I work that tomorrow when I deliver something, I go to that organization, people should remember me for something. She stood up for what she believed in and delivered. And WOW. We did not think of this **first**. That's how I work.

My job is subject matter expertise, but still if that is not in line with the organization's objectives or thought process, and everybody has a point of view then plainly there are too many cooks in the broth, and that broth is spoilt.

When you look at your peers who do you identify with more? women or men?
Wow, that's a tricky one. Actually, I will not go down the sexist route on this. I come from the fact that I know things and I don't know anything. My motto in life is listen, learn, do, unlearn, listen, learn. I don't care if you were a management trainee, you're a man, woman or whatever gender nowadays are, if you can teach me something, sure, let's roll with it. Instead of gender classifying my approach, I would call it a direct approach. I don't know whether men use it more or women. This is the approach I have adopted what has worked for me.

What do you think is the most ideal dress for women in the workplace?
According to me it depends from organization to organization. But I think you should have a sense of unique style, your own

authentic blend. So, if you are soft, then wear pastel colours, a sari or a modern combination. If you are aggressive and like to walk into the room, get noticed then dress sharply, no bling. You dress as if you are in business, because you're not going for a party. You're going to sit on a table. I, for example, if I had to go for a very senior meeting, would I wear a business suit like men do, then the answer is no. I would wear a sari, but an unconventional one. I'll wear a very modern looking blouse. I will have huge makeup, no flashy rings or whatever. I'll wear my serious glasses, because then you got to play the part, right? But I also have my quirks and I don't compensate for my quirks. My nature, my behavior doesn't change but my dressing style changes. You can't have the same dressing style, everywhere. I just think that for women it is a package and sum total of all - your behavior, your dress.

My favourite quote is, be who you are and be that well.

Marriage & Career or Marriage vs Career? What are your views? Do you think one has to sacrifice their career for marriage? Does marriage have anything to do with feeling fulfilled in life?
I've been married. I made mistakes in my life. Personally, I find what our parents don't teach us is **Individuality**. We're told. We never learn to stand up for own selves and say No.

Nobody thinks twice about giving a promotion to a man when he is leaving, but not a woman when she is leaving. These are all set standards which nobody questions. Today organizations talk about maternal and paternal leave and women's equality, but do they follow it in spirit?

After all people change every day, they buy new phones, they watch latest movies, meet people, travel, they learn, they adapt. But learning new things, to adapt to new behavioural norms they don't want to do. Nothing can be done. I know so many men who have wives who are homemakers. At work, they are so aggressive, but when they go back home, they're passive aggressive. I know so many women also who are like that.

Adaptability comes from standing up in the right points in life. I mean today, if I'm getting married, to take my own example, I was very clear in my head. I have a career, I earn a living, I can be a woman of the house, but I'm not here to earn and cook food for you. You share the load. A Marriage is a union of two people, not one person. I think most women forget that. Women think they are the only ones who have to make sacrifices. I know it's very tough one. I can empathize with that.

There are times women have to say, hey, I have a child, I want to focus on my child, I will take a lesser portfolio, Sure, allow her that. Or hey, I want to take a larger role, I'm ready. My child has support or I will make the arrangements. That is how you make a marriage successful, right? Both make compromises.

That's precisely what most women **don't** do. They fail to set up the mark of what they want, what they don't want. Because they get into that zone of peacemakers, they let it go on as long as the trappings are there of a "good life".

Woman, you are the only driver of your bus. If you don't have control over the bus, nobody else can. People are going to only tell you to go left or right, but the turn you have to take. Equality doesn't mean asking for equal rights. It's not a movement. It means stand up for yourself, drive your bus, change your attitude, behavior. Become the driver, not the passenger. Start with your own home, in your own surroundings.

Do you think women's attitude will change in India? In every home?
Of course, of course. The biggest example is, why do you think there are so many divorces happening? Today there are 9 million single women in India. Why are they happening? Because women are getting more educated, they're having more exposure, they're going out in the world and saying hey my life can be better. They have tips from other women, if not, they are seeing, they have exposure, even if they have to come back home, even if the situation might be difficult. Sometimes they continue to tolerate because of children or because they are supporting parents. They say I'll be better off by myself.

The women have evolved, they have changed. Changed from the nurturer, homemaker, or how do you say, from the subdued one, to I want to have the balance of it all. Whereas men are exactly where they are. It is only because they have not grown in this journey. That's the dichotomy here. They are exactly where they were.

I have so many men friends in my own social circle, they want a good-looking friend to hang with, drink, eat or whatever but when they get married, they want a gharelu (domesticated) girl. These are all educated people. I say education has got nothing to do with how you think. Because women are now raising a voice, because women are out there breaking the glass ceiling, so things are changing.

The diving story
Whenever I would go for a shoot, so when I would go for setting up all the equipment and individual gear, the guys on the boat would say like what, why are you doing this, carrying this heavy weight of the oxygen tank? They'll be like, oh, we're

not saying that because you are a woman but I know that's what it means. I would pick up my own tank and I would do the work with all the boys. I was trained like that. Where I came from and where I was trained there was no sex. Man, Woman, whatever. Do what you got to do.

It's like a calling. I didn't know it was my calling till actually it came. It showed itself to me. When I made this choice, it was just to learn another skill set and that's when I quit my job, took up diving. It was something to learn, a skill set I didn't know, I didn't know I'll be India's second female master scuba diver trainer. I literally just took to water, it was love for water, ocean. I am a nature person. I love it. I was like, whoa, this is something I would love to know. It's delving into the unknown. I didn't know that 70% of the earth is underwater which we never even see. The thrill of being able to discover that just by learning a skill enthralled me. And when you immerse yourself into something, you learn new things. I realized who I am, an empath and that if I really want to make a change, then it begins with me.

I decided that until I know what is water, what it does for us, till I become a subject matter expert, I will not teach. I've never been a champion swimmer, I learnt from scratch. Learning how to dive, going into the ocean, respecting the ocean, learning from it and unlearning many things was the journey. I became a student, surrendered to the ocean and said to it, I know nothing.

In that vast spectrum of things, we are like a little tiny speck. We can only go with the flow, absorb and grow. I always believe that the ocean heals, it gives a lot of grace.

It gave me the strength to break down, to respect life, its processes, the small and big things.

I have seen that every time I learn something new, the

universe opened its path for me. Whether it was to become MSDT (Master Scuba Diving Trainer), to get a diving job in India, to teach with the fabulous diving schools, to shoot films. Who imagined that those possibilities were there? I didn't even know that, you can teach in India or I didn't even know that you could shoot for films or be a part of a crew, which shoots for films, underwater. Possibilities just unfolded. I am a person who always challenges herself with something which is extraordinary and unknown. That's when I get the adrenaline rush.

As I went along that path, I realized I was good at it. It was a spiritual process, which left me filled with gratitude.

Hullo Kanika, how are you doing? I understand there is a new challenge in your life?
I am good. One day at a time. My life becomes exciting every time I say, oh, this is it; something new happens. I am so much better than I was. I don't get into small jams, only big storms for me. My friends ask me, couldn't you have broken a leg, instead you got cancer. It is malignant.

I loved that, whether it was empathy, or whether it was taking a dive. I don't know. To me it was equal, either you surrender and you accept life's challenges with grace. Then the path will be clear to you.

I'm not alone. I'm blessed with so many friends, I'm almost like a film star. I've had all my girlfriends standing with me. I go to the hospital with over 10 people. I have flowers in my house that it looks like a garden. I have so many people praying for me, sending me healing. So, I'm actually feeling so overwhelmed, I must have done some right karma in my life. Or I was just very lucky.

So much of love and affection I didn't even know I had.

It was difficult, initially. I was in shock. Took me a while to accept it. But here I am.

I was in that space in my life where I realized this is not how I want to lead my life, running after money, chasing a designation. I have done all those by the grace of God. I said no matter what, I will be there. I'm just going to take the leap of faith. I did that and I've never felt sorry, ever.

Believe me, it doesn't even bog me down that I have cancer. It really doesn't. My first question to the doctor was when can I dive? She just looked at me after five minutes of tears and said, well, you are worried about diving.

I am in remission since 2023. In Dec 2023 I dove first time with tiger sharks, finally uniting with my beloved ocean and sharks. When I dunk my head in the ocean after 2 years of treatment, it was a big moment for me. It was overwhelming. I was thankful to the universe, for life lived to the fullest. If tomorrow was the day, I had to shut my eye and never wake up. I have done it all. I think that amounts to having lived a life with the right set of choices. Good, bad, ugly, whatever, but I will never do it another way.

"My take on
Kanika Saxena

Her upbringing

Kanika's interview comes as a surprise after nine in a row showcasing a "normal" secure childhood. With her topsy turvy childhood, it becomes easy to appreciate the impact a stable life can have on a child's life. 80% of the girls in India are caught between "Indian Culture" and their own perception of 21st century India. Kanika was lucky she had the means, support and the courage and determination to get out when she could. 100% of the 80% don't. But it is not the stats which is the point here but her hard work, persistence, Zen like focus on her goal and her "finding herself" which took her to become- India's 2nd Woman Master Suba Diving trainer.

I am indebted to her for sharing her story so that the 90 lakh women can learn from it. And therefore, I will humbly point out what I want the girls to take away.

Like any typical youngster – boy or girl, she has taken up Media as her career with her limited knowledge, to avoid being married off. This is called the avoidance strategy. But Scuba Diving she has taken when "I had to stop to understand what was going on?". She ran away underwater from her 2nd marriage and was fascinated by the world she saw there. She calls Scuba Diving her "calling". And she is using all the qualities she already has in her to master her one true love.

Millions stuck in unsatisfying jobs must learn from her – even if you are doing what you don't enjoy, don't miss out on the opportunity to be the best at it. You never know when your "true love" will turn up. The high standards she sets for herself and the way she drives herself to achieve them, is her innate approach to anything she sets her heart and mind to do, be it Media or Diving.

Hermann Hesse once said that the true profession of a man is a way to find himself. I think Kanika has found herself. Her approach is a learned skill and her leadership is millions of nuggets she has for the women of today.

Kanika today is fighting cancer since a few months after we did this interview. She did achieve her goal for going diving in Sept 2022 as her cancer is in remission, surprising her doctors.

All of us as parents, bosses and colleagues need to respect a woman's "NO" because we don't know what or who she could be fighting with. IF Being called a rebel is the only price to pay for doing what you love to do, then embrace that label. Labels can change. Just like Kanika's did. India's Woman Scuba Diving Trainer.

Wish you loads of good health Kanika.

Sanju Yadav
MARKETING HEAD, MSN LABS

SHEER ACADEMIC COMMITMENT and determination to fulfil her father's dream, brought to life by her mother's fighting spirit, helped Sanju realize her dreams against all odds, especially coming from a remote village in Bihar. Everybody at home knew that the girl will go far because she was intelligent. She didn't make it to medical in her first attempt but while preparing for her 2nd attempt, she started enjoying college life so much that she decided to continue doing bachelor in science and prepare for MBA instead. The college was Miranda House at Delhi University, so one can understand.

Medicine's loss was Pharma's gain. Today she is heading marketing excellence at MSN Labs. With 18 years of Sales and Marketing and 2.5 years of business unit leadership experience, she is one of the few pharma professionals who have worked both in leading Multinational as well as Indian companies, big & small. Here is an overview of her industry experience:

- Presently with MSN Laboratories as Head – Marketing excellence.
- 6 months (Jan – Jun 2021), MSD Pharmaceuticals, Senior Manager Marketing.

- 1 year (Aug 2019 -Jul 2020), Samarth Lifesciences, Business Unit Head, Women's Health Care.
- 1-year 5m (Sep 2017 – Jan 2019), Alembic Pharmaceuticals, Division Head, Gastroenterology.
- 6 years 6 Months (March 2011 – Aug 2017), Pfizer Ltd, Therapy Lead, Marketing.
- 4 years 4 months (Nov 2006 – Feb 2011) Merck KGaA, Group Product Manager.
- 1 year 3 months (Aug 2005 – Oct 2006) Glenmark Pharmaceuticals, Product Manager.
- 1 year 1 month (Jul 2004 – Jul 2005), Cipla Ltd, Product Manager.
- 2 years 2 months (May 2002 – June 2004), Charak Pharma, Product Manager.

Charak gave her healing career a start, by training her in the field, and she landed up in pharmaceutical product management, a field which felt "right" for her. She is continuing her interest in healing therapies through Yoga, NLP and contributing in the pharma industry. I have no doubt that her students in the B. Pharm class of NMIMS will be studying Pharma from the perspective of "wellness rather than an illness" (in Sanju's words) perspective. We will wait to see her magic in her healing potions.

- Post Graduate Diploma in Business Administration (PGDBA), Institute for Technology & Management (ITM Business school), Kharghar (2000-2002)
- B.Sc. (Hons), Botany, Miranda House, University of Delhi (1997-2000)
- Advanced Certificate in Digital Marketing, IIDE, 2022
- Certified Yoga instructor, The Yoga Institute and AYUSH, Govt. of India, 2019

- Diploma in NLP. Certified NLP Coach, NLP coaching academy, 2019
- Leadership development program from IIM, Ahmedabad, 2017
- Certificate course in Emotional Intelligence, FEIL, 2016

Sat, 11/6 9:55PM • 1:00:57

Were you brought up in a joint family or a nuclear family?
I live in Mumbai now, but I'm originally from a village known as Kharjhakhiya in Bihar. From Patna it is six hours, geographically. It is a very remote village, which got electricity only few years back. I was born in a middle-class joint family. My parents came from an uneducated background, in a manner of speaking. But my father was very enterprising. He educated himself, learnt a foreign language, picked up accounting skills. That helped him gain employment in Bhutan. He started as a teenager, then somehow got in touch with the royal family of Bhutan. He got employed there working in their retail outlet, and later on grew to become the manager of the outlet. At some point he became influential, that's when our fortunes changed. He grew very quickly. By the time I was 10 years old, we were financially well off. He was family oriented, so he took over the responsibility of managing the entire family, including his two brothers and several sister's marriages. We lived in a joint family where my father was the sole bread earner. All the kid's education was very, very important for him. He invested time and effort in educating everybody, all the kids of all the three brothers, fourteen to be precise. Educationally, my generation did not suffer.

When I was five years old, I went to Bhutan. That's where my primary education started, in Thimphu, which is the capital of Bhutan. I had just finished my primary education when my father passed away. I was 11 years old then. We had to move back from Thimphu to the border of India and Bhutan, which is Phuentsholing and Jaigaon. We have a house there now. We have our agricultural land base in Bihar since agriculture is also our family profession.

That's the background – I am third among four brothers and sisters.

What was the family environment like where you grew up?
My mother was not educated. Even as a housewife, she was very protected, was not the decision maker in the house. My uncle took over the reins in terms of managing the house and the family business, after my father's demise. We had property, but money wise, we didn't know how much money we had. She had no inkling about bank accounts, or anything like that. My father was unwell for 10 days, and then suddenly he passed away. My mother had come to the village for some work so they could not even have that final meeting at the end.

Money wise, my mother was clueless to start with. My father had also lent money to a lot of people. People used to just come up on their own to return the money they had taken. Financially we really did not have a problem as such, but emotionally my mother had to fight a lot to give us a good living.

For one year, she was completely clueless, grieving, kind of depressed, not living actively, just lying somewhere. She did look after us, but very sad, grieving. Before my Class 10 my uncle got my sister married off at a young age. For him it was a responsibility he was ticking off. My mother was not very involved at that time. But by the time I was in my 9th / 10th, she became actively involved. She started taking decisions about us. Because my father had this dream of educating us and making us independent. Especially for me, he wanted me to be a doctor. Everybody including me wanted me to be a doctor.

My dad's desire was to provide equal education to all children. Whoever was good in studies, he would give them better treatment. His bias was towards education and intelligence, not gender. But my mother, she came from village background, personally she definitely had that bias between boy and girl. I'm just reflecting that if we had had a resource crunch, the girls would have suffered. That's the background I come from.

Which school did you study in? Were there good schools around?
I went to a private school, Air Force School, CBSE board. We were all educated in good schools, like my brother went to St. Paul's School in Darjeeling, which is, again, one of the best residential schools in India. He along with my other male cousins, all went there. My father wanted to send me to a girl's residential school. Unfortunately, that could not happen.

After Class 10, I went to Patna for my plus two. I did very well in studies and got a decent 87% which got me admission in Delhi University for graduation along with hostel. As long as doors were opening, my family did not pull us back. They always pushed us. I saw other families, really well to do, but they would not send their daughters far away for studies, be it Delhi or Bombay or Calcutta. But my mother did not have that kind of thought process. If my marks were good, if I secured admission, then definitely she would help and push.

What was school life like? Who were you in school - The teacher's pet, the class bully or the back bencher? How did that shape you?

I was the teacher's pet, as I used to come first. My family's favourite, my father's for sure. He was very proud of me. Every time the mark sheet was expected, there used to be celebrations, in preparation for my results. I would come first. Somehow, I was positively pressured with an urge to always give my best and do well. I was raised with a lot of praise and positivity. It encouraged me to be well behaved. I don't remember struggles in my childhood at all, except for missing my dad very much. I was also good in debates and in elocution. I used to take part in all of that. I was not very sports oriented. But did well in extra-curricular as well as academics.

How did you deal with the cultural difference between Delhi and your home town?

Yeah, it was definitely good exposure, but then see, I had lived in Thimphu also. Personally, I don't really feel like I had come from a small place to a big place. I was quite comfortable in the hostel. Hostel is again protected; it is certainly more protective than living in Delhi as a day scholar.

Hostelites all came from outside Delhi. There were a lot of different cultures. I did not really feel out of place. Right from the beginning, I was comfortable. I think travelling in childhood and exposure to different countries, states and culture helped.

When did you start thinking about who or what you want to become? Is there any particular incident which was the turning point – which influenced your career choice?

Basically, I wanted to be a doctor. After plus two, I did give the medical entrance exams. There was AIIMS and a central examination. I gave both but I did not clear. Then there were two options before me. One was to just go for college and keep preparing; two take a break, to prepare. Somehow, I felt that I should go to college. I joined Miranda House, science stream, with the thought of preparing for Medical. There were other girls also who were exercising similar options. But once I started preparing, two to three months down the line, I started enjoying college life. My mind started opening up in terms of other options. Till now I was not aware of anything apart from being a doctor or engineer. There were many things one could do. That was the time India was at the forefront internationally. I was quite kicked about taking MBA as a stream. I was completely engrossed in college life in my last year, on getting through MBA.

I gave CAT exam. Through CAT I got Institute of Technology and Management (ITM) interview. There was Group Discussion (GD) and interview at Delhi. Then once I secured my admission, I had to come to Mumbai in June. In my family, nobody had ever come to Mumbai. It was a big deal and I was considered a trail blazer.

Where did you acquire your professional education and training? What was your thinking process when you chose this as your career?
It was on Campus. I did a general MBA. While doing my MBA, I was more interested in getting into the travel industry or into the FMCG sectors or banking. My friends were more inclined towards banking while I was inclined towards travel and FMCG. I did my summer internship in Jones Lang LaSalle, which is a real estate company. By the time I finished my MBA, because I was a science grad, companies that were offering placement were pharma companies. Once you clear an interview you cannot refuse an offer. The choice was somewhat made for me.

2002 was a recession kind of a year though recession did not affect India that much. It was more widespread in the US. There were a lot of experienced people in India looking for jobs. It was difficult to get one. I got offers from Wockhardt & Charak; I accepted Charak. I really didn't know much about Pharma industry. It wasn't like I chose Pharma, but pharma chose me, because I had a science background. Once I started working in the pharma industry, I never thought about leaving it.

Did it have any influence on your personality or your career opportunities?
I joined pharma in marketing because I had majored in marketing. I had studied brand management which is the core of marketing. Between the two options - Wockhardt and Charak, Wockhardt was a bigger company, well established. They wanted me to join as a medical rep, not even a Management Trainee. Based on my performance I could move in product management later.

Charak was not like that. I got the role of a product executive, where I had to be on the field for one year as part of training. Post that I was to be placed in product management. For me it was a tough call to make in terms of a small company, better role vs a big company, sales role.

To start with I did not really know much about what a medical rep does. I hadn't ever really seen a medical representative before; everything I came to know after entering the industry. In my family also, there was no connection to service. Mostly people had their own business or were into agriculture. I really did not know anything about the different functions or any other profession for that matter. The decision became easy as I wanted to utilize my marketing skills straightaway with a management role.

Once I joined Charak, I was able to do brand management. There was a sales stint, where I had to work in the field with a medical representative and do sales calls. It was interesting, I could see the light, I mean the whole medical representative's plan. Being based in the head office, I would get good conversations with the customers/ doctors. Within three months, the company decided that I should get into a proper product management role. I started managing brands in head office.

The role complimented me very well, it suited my nature at that point of time, it was a good fit. I never felt any problem in terms of what I was doing or that I wanted to be somebody else. No such thoughts came to my mind ever in my career. My focus was always on excelling at the job at hand.

What will be your advice to young women about to commence their career?
Whether career or life, I think to make a decision, one has to look at all the options, weigh them properly. One should listen to everybody, but finally do what really comes from their heart. I tend to listen to my heart more than my brain. Though I'm a thinker kind of person, I do weigh my options and everything. And finally, I listen to my heart. I believe that is really the true essence of happiness, to follow your heart. Also Focus on living your present to the fullest, whether at work or in Life.

In the Banking industry many women have kicked headlines big time. But in the Indian pharma industry, I can actually think of Kiran Mazumdar Shah or Anu Agha only. Am I missing somebody?
You are absolutely right; they are also founders, not employees who have climbed ranks. Pharma is a conservative industry and seems to be a follower in Diversity & inclusion and not

a leader. Though currently things are changing for the better.

From whom did you imbibe your early leadership lessons? And what was that?
I am influenced by my father. I always had lot of respect and love for him subconsciously. I contemplated a lot on my father's life and way of "being", later at a conscious level. I was very much influenced by the way he conducted things, how he was respected by everybody around him, for his contribution to our entire family. The huge positive impact, that he really created on the entire family of more than 20 people. As a person he really valued truth and honesty. That is something which came very strongly in me right from childhood. I remember a lot of stories where, in normal circumstances, a child would lie to avert a beating or a shouting but I never did that. My mom tells me there were many times I could have just lied and got away with it, but even at the cost of getting beaten, I would never lie.

That firmed up my beliefs about how to raise your child with praise and positivity, I think that works with me. It made life simpler. That is one value, which I've got from my father. Anything may happen, but he would never lie. I learned to value that. And it has served me very well.

Did the India culture ever prove to be a hindrance to you? If so, when? If not, then what is your secret in handling it?
In the early days, I was very much encouraged by my seniors. I was spotted to be a star performer, much appreciated and recognized for my work. Everything was very good and came easily to me in the early phase of my career. The first two years at Charak, I remember I got four increments and one promotion. At a young age I was given the responsibility to manage the

entire corporate branding, to launch brands. I hardly had actual experience, though at that time I didn't feel like that. That's very ironical. Now I have 18 years of experience, but even when I had one year of experience, I never felt that I didn't have experience. But it's only looking back that I have added 18 years of experience but at no point of time, I felt immature or that I'm not yet ready. That confidence took me from the Ayurvedic category to the mainstream Allopathic one. That's how I moved to Cipla, the No.1 pharma company in India at that time in 2004. At Cipla also I did well, I got an early confirmation with a letter of appreciation in the first six months.

Cipla was again a very unconventional company. I had good opportunity to launch brands, good environment. The founder, Mr. Hamid's leadership style had a great influence on me in the beginning of my career. He was a very humble person. It touched my heart and has stayed with me as a lesson for life. Even as the owner of Cipla which was the number one company in the entire country in terms of sales turnover, he would sit in the same chair as everybody, on the same floor, in the same way exactly, like everybody else. He wanted it like that. That had a great influence on me in terms of how a person should be. I remember when his daughter was getting married, they had a reception at The Taj Palace.

Everybody got a personal invitation. The language was very personal, he used his pet name to sign the card. His name was MK Hamid, M, I think stands for Mustafa. But in the card, he had written Mukoo and Buloo. Buloo was his wife. When I read that I felt valued. That is a lesson that's really remained with me, of how you can touch people, how you can really connect with people, by being yourself, by just being humble. He was sixty-five years old, and had lots of energy, humility, enthusiasm and was always lively. That stayed with me as a lesson and an early role model.

With Glenmark I learnt that influencing was the way you're doing things, networking and having good relationships with peers. Merck Serono was the first MNC in my career. In terms of culture, definitely there was a cultural shift from Indian companies. Employee Orientation was much, much higher for Merck Serono. That was the first time I was given a team to manage.

Was there anything in your corporate environment which in your journey as a woman leader, you could say are encouraging factors and restraining factors?

In the beginning, I did feel that there was a certain personality, which was conducive to leading, which was more of a masculine personality. I saw that women who were actually leading were changing into this masculine version of themselves. Those are the role models which were available to me at that time. I've never seen feminity being celebrated or talked about. Every aggressive woman would do well. Maybe I was also aggressive at that time. I was in the mould.

That is how, maybe I did well, at that point in time. In my mind, gender and all that inequality was never there. I never felt that I was marginalized as a woman. I don't have a recollection of that feeling. It was more about meritocracy. If somebody is performing well, they were given recognition and opportunities. Of course, I had not become a mother yet. I was a go getter kind of a personality. That helped with that phase of my career. When I was pregnant, I had a woman boss which helped a little bit, but my entire peer group was male. That's the time when I started seeing a little shift in terms of people's expectations. In my work life, I have always been surrounded by 80% men and very few women. In Sales it is worse, it is 5% women and 95% men.

When I'm working, I tend to forget other things in my life. That much of focus I used to bring to my job. Traveling was becoming a bit difficult. In terms of support, the company and my boss, my peers, everybody supported me. I was working till 7 - 8 o'clock in the evening, reaching home by nine or later. I did not make any change. Had I not done that, if I wanted to leave at 5-6 o'clock, I'm aware it would not have been supported. Somehow, now, looking back at that time, I did not feel the need to do that. As a young woman of 28, when a woman gets pregnant and if she decides to leave by five o'clock, heavens will fall. People pay lip service to supporting women.

Till now I have not seen action on the ground. Even in my last assignment, a D & I pro company- did not have policies and support for D & I. Needs of the family is not a valid reason for taking leave.

Meritocracy is only a concept. Women have to work doubly hard, at home as well as in office. Yet they have to adhere to the same judgement scale as men, in fact worse with all those sub conscious biases and blind spots of men around especially in leadership roles. Women don't get any leeway that they have children or a family. Family expects you to be home on time, but companies expect you to sit late, to "show" how committed you are.

However successful a woman is, the natural expectation is that she is the primary caregiver, the primary nurturer of the family; even if you have maids, but the boss at home is the woman. That is the expectation. If you want a really fulfilling career, you need very strong family support especially from husband. The biggest decision is not the company you work for, but the life partner you choose. Otherwise, it's really difficult for women to do well in their careers.

How do you put across a viewpoint which you know is conflicting with that of a male dominated group?
In terms of the ideas that you bring as an individual, whether it is a man or a woman, getting the ideas implemented, I have not really faced any discrimination. But yeah, I've never really experienced any support also. All talk of how to get women back into the workforce, how to support them, that they are able to manage their work life better. I have not really seen actions in practice. In practice, it is the same, whether it's a man or a woman, workplace expectations and support are the same.

What do you think is the ideal professional dress for women at the workplace?
That is one lesson I've learned from living in Patna, Bhutan and traveling all over India. It's a lesson that was spoken by my family also. Jaisa Desh, Waisa Bhesh (as a nation, so the dress). It is not advisable to stand out in a negative way. One should always strive to stand out in a positive way, be the best dressed in that sense. Every company has a different culture, in terms of dressing also, one needs to understand the norm and balance it with their personality and personal needs.

Skin show is a sensitive area and one has to be professional in every company as per their cultural norms. One tends to understand what is okay, what is not. For American companies, the dress code is more formal but in European companies, the dress code is very informal. They wear feminine attire like blouses, dresses and tops. I have been in Merck Serono which is an open organization, that feminine look was appreciated. A woman looks like a woman. In India salwar kameez comes in handy. I like to be dressed well but not make my clothes the highlights because people get distracted. I wear a variety of clothes but professionally I stick to something which is comfortable with the audience.

On the field I mostly wear salwar kameez.

Marriage & Career or Marriage or Career? What are your views? Do you think one has to sacrifice their career for marriage? Does marriage have anything to do with feeling fulfilled in life?

I definitely believe that marriage is a very big life decision. I personally am in favour of marriage of your own choice. Because if you choose your own partner, I think one has better ability to deal with a lot of things which may not go your way, because there are many unknown factors. I believe to have good balance of marriage with career, the partner and the partner's family plays a key role, especially when the kids come. Since the woman has to leave her home, if you have family members breathing down your neck, it's difficult to concentrate on your work. Apart from Bombay, Delhi and the bigger cities in India, the culture is still where mother-in-law is the boss of the house. The woman comes into the family, she has to adjust to the family. It can be tough to focus the way it is required in a career.

One has to be really lucky. Touchwood, I was lucky enough, I had a love marriage. My mother-in-law is not demanding in terms of what I should do or should not do. Things just happened to work out. I am family oriented and their wellbeing is a priority. Career becomes a BIG decision. Because then the whole question of financial security of the whole family becomes critical. If the family is not very financially secure, then she may choose to continue. It's not really driven very much by the desire of the woman wanting to work, it is more a financial decision.

Women dropout, mostly when their husbands are doing

very well; or they have good financial security from the family side. Or they may drop out if they have tough working conditions.

They tend to stay if the boss is also good, and environment is not very stressful.

But after a kid, it's a big crossroad for every woman, what she really wants to do. For me also it was the same. I had extended maternity leave. Thankfully I got like, five to six months of maternity leave. But after six months also, you have to live with that guilt. Especially during that breastfeeding period, it is like the daily reminder to pump and throw the milk. It does take an emotional toll on you. Financial security was also one of the reasons why I stayed on. And my job was fulfilling, my family very supportive. Things worked out very well for me as I had only one child. With more kids, the complications only increase and becomes more difficult for women to continue. I don't have any bad memories about going back to work except for mom guilt.

There is a logistical issue involved, in looking after the children as offices are far from home. From your practical experience anything the government can do which can make it easier for women to continue with their jobs?

Yes, I think office creches is something which is a very, very important thing. I remember, if I had a creche, I would have been happier. That separation anxiety is there definitely. Because you're occupied with your work, you tend to push it down, but then it lingers in your subconscious. Definitely, it has a role to play in your overall wellbeing. I think Creche is something which could be a boon for women, not being dependent on some private creche. If you can just go and attend to the child throughout the day. They don't need you

24 hours, right. A few minutes here and there would make a lot of difference. One can manage work better. Creche is something which I did not have, in any of my companies. I think it would have been a great value addition.

Apart from Creche, flexibility in work time. When I was a new mother, we did not have flexibility as a concept. Today, because of Corona, at least flexibility has come into the forefront and people are understanding the value of it, even for a man. Flexibility doesn't eliminate many problems; it just means really deciding value for your time. For a woman, it would be a game changer. If a woman can manage her time if she can work from home, and can be around to fulfil her family obligations along with work, that would be the best.

That is still not there in the corporate world.

Now about you, what do you like doing, how do you renew yourself? What makes you angry?
As a person, I am quite fun loving, positive and optimistic. Even in bad situations, I don't get bogged down by the circumstances, I have this natural ability to see the good in that situation, which makes me come across as a strong personality. I've been told that I am dynamic and bold because I come from that background. India is paternalistic as a society. Women just doing what they want to do, is seen as bold, though it is just being normal. But definition of a strong woman is very funny, because a strong woman is somebody who asserts herself. An individual is actually supposed to assert her/himself. You'll never say a strong man, because the man has always asserted himself. But whenever a woman asserts herself, she's called strong woman and if doesn't, then she's called woman. I think that gap is still there in the overall societal make up.

What motivates me is continuous learning. Thanks to

that I have grown a lot as an individual.

I've always been inclined to read a lot. I've got a lot of training in all of the companies that I've worked with. I have taken initiative to ask for courses, which the companies have allowed. Just reading a book makes me happy.

As for renewing myself, I have varied interests. I love cooking, reading, painting. I'm excited about life and work. There are many things which the new me can do. I like yoga. I'm not much into exercising, I don't like going to gym. I'm not a very outdoor person in terms of running and all that, but yoga is something I really like. Having met with an accident where I broke my knee-cap and had to take a career break for better rehab and recovery has really made me value health and wellness above everything in life.

Coming back to your peer group, in your opinion what do you think is a mistake which most working women make?
When I was younger, I felt that maybe there is a little bit of risk aversion, with women. It could be the country culture. In fact, I too never looked at sales as an option for me, like most women. But the men were not like that. They would jump at a sales role, because that would help them grow to the next level but for women I think, it is a big decision. It was mostly No.

I never wanted to lead the sales organization, though I did want to become a leader of people. After my marketing stint, as a business unit head, I got over my reluctance of managing sales. I would have never thought of applying for a sales head role earlier, but it changed with exposure and I am more comfortable with a sales role now. But it came only after a while. Personally, I don't see marketing and sales as separate when it comes to leadership. It is important to understand the core of what you want and not get distracted by many paths which could lead to your coveted destination. For me, my passion now is leadership which offers me an opportunity to make a difference in the lives of many people. That motivates me daily.

As far as your peers are concerned how would you like them to remember you?
I have done a lot of contemplation. In my past, I've asked all my peers for their feedback, just to make myself a better person. I think it is in line with what I think, I've not really been surprised with their feedback. I know how the world views me and how I view myself, is more or less the same. They can remember me the way they would like to based on my words, actions and behavior.

Do you want to do anything differently going forward?
Basically, I listen to my heart. I take decisions after carefully thinking but then finally, I listen to my heart. That is why I think looking back, I don't have regrets as such. I'm quite happy with all my decisions.

But in terms of work life balance and really understanding, there are certain things you learn as you evolve or by experience. The pandemic experience itself has taught us so much, a knowledge which was always available in books, but the learning was not as deep as when it actually struck. Most importantly is the focus on health. I think that is something which I never had earlier.

I've not really invested in keeping myself healthy at all. I've got into that preventive mindset. Taking action on the preventive work, adopting yoga or eating better, for nutrition. But I think one should keep it right, in the beginning and be health and life conscious from an early age. Till the age of 38, I really never bothered about health. That is something which

I, now when I look back, I would like to correct.

Now I feel very passionately about health. It is in our hands only, I feel very passionate about wellness and prevention, rather than treatment. That is something which I think is a major change that has happened in the last 4-5 years. More so in the last two to three years.

Pharma is an industry of illness. Wellness is something that we should aspire for. So that would make my current industry obsolete and make way for a whole new way of looking at and managing health where technology will also play a major enabler. More power to the future!

My take on Sanju Yadav

Upbringing

Sanju's upbringing though dotted by upheavals, has been well managed by her mother and inspired by her father's dreams for her. When I read Sanju's interview, I am reminded of the maxim, "All roads lead to Rome". From a young age, wanting to be a doctor but then not getting that subject, she changed her subject choice and still ended up in the healer's shoes, creating therapies, instead of administering them. That shows resilience, perhaps imbibed from her mother, who did not drop the parenting ball after her husband's demise, brought up four children, providing that solid foundation for Sanju to live her dreams.

Her Career

Sanju's desire to come first always, has defined her expectations from herself, which is evident in her successful tenure in the first 3 jobs, as an individual contributor. She has taken initiative and shown what she is capable of, as evident from the quick promotions she got initially. She was clear in what she wanted to become, though her route (subjects) may have changed along the way. Her passion for leadership and health is clearly evident in her life choices.

Leadership
She works from the heart and right now she may be a round peg in a square hole because functional competency and revenue generation rule the roost in pharma. The deliberate way in which she has gone about imbibing leadership and choosing her role models with care, is definitely out of the "mould". That she is a woman to watch out for, is evident from her potent analysis of the pharma industry, that it should be "wellness focused rather than illness focused".

Women specific
There is a telling point in Sanju's narrative where she mentions about corporate reality being opposite of family expectations. That becomes a stumbling block, in my view. So, either reality has to change or expectations have to change if this patriarchal society wants to see its women realize their potential.

An industry which runs on scientific discoveries and patents, why there is a gender skew is still a mystery. Unlike the West, where efforts are made to attract young girls into STEM (Science, technology, engineering, and mathematics) careers, minimal efforts are made to attract girls to a Pharma career, in India. This is despite India being the leading provider of capable and well qualified pharma talent to the world; though gender skewed.

Anuradha Deb
FOUNDER PROCESS WORK
INSTITUTE OF INDIA (PWII)

ANURADHA DEB I have known Anuradha for almost 12 years now. Though her entry into my life was marked by personal upheavals, which had nothing to do with her, but her listening, advising, insights, pushing and talking helped me deal with the upheavals. And having been in the same profession, I had zero understanding of what her work is about. After attending a couple of her workshops, I began to understand the difference between the process she talks about and the process in corporate parlance. In very language, the processing we do internally, of emotions, to deal with them, is her forte. I am glad I was able to squeeze in her interview just before this book went into publishing.

She is also a corporate coach and trained psychotherapist with 25 years of experience, an active member of ISABS. She offers corporate consultancy at the national and international levels under the aegis of **Anuradha Deb & Associates, Mumbai.** Her HR expertise combined with her knowledge of human behavior has enabled her to make path breaking, pioneering interventions in a wide horizon of fields like **Process Consulting, Talent management, Employee development, Organisational Health and diagnostics.**

She has a wide portfolio which has a diverse spectrum,

at national and international forums. **She is a member of an international team of Process Consultants who offer training in Conflict Management and Sustainable Community building at seminars internationally.**

Anuradha is the only Indian certified Psychotherapist in her field of specialization. She is well known in the field of mental health having a large practice which she offers to private as well as corporate clients.

She is the principal trustee and founder of the **Process work Institute of India, Mumbai, which is a school for training therapists and counselors. (Go to: www.pwindia.com).**

She is President of Governing Board of Global Process Institute, Portland USA, works with conflict areas globally for peace building initiatives.

Besides an MSc (Developmental Psychology) from Jadavpur University, Calcutta and a B.Ed. from the same university, Anuradha has certified herself in:

- Certificate in Personal Counseling, Xavier's Institute of counseling, Mumbai.
- MA, Process Oriented Psychology, Process Work Centre of Portland, Oregon State, USA.
- PG Diploma in Process Oriented Psychology, PWCP, Oregon Sate, USA.
- ICF certified transformational coach .
- Professional Member, Indian Society of Applied Behavioral Sciences, New Delhi.
- Certification in all Psychometric tests as well as Management Profiling from SHL
- Certification in Thomas Profiling.

Thanks Anuradha for finding that burst of energy to give this valuable interview. Read it here:

Oct 19 at 11:37 PM

What about your upbringing? Was it a joint family or nuclear?
We were basically a nuclear family but functioned more like a large joint family. I lived with my brother and my parents. My father was in the Indian army, in Military Engineering Service. We were transferred every three years. There was a lot of movement and we ended up growing mostly in small cities of Uttar Pradesh and Madhya Pradesh. Then finally I completed my schooling in Meerut and Delhi.

The joint family influence was that my father had eleven brothers and three sisters. And so till my grandmother was alive, she lived with one of the brothers. The joint family aspect was predominant that whenever the family met for a wedding, or a funeral or any family event, everybody came to where my grandmother was. All the brothers came and so we never needed anybody from outside. Whenever we had holidays, we went back to where the family was at that time.

My grandfather had died when I was about three or four years old. When he passed away, the younger siblings were still in school. So, the elder brothers then took over financial responsibility of bringing up their younger siblings. That had a major influence on the family dynamics as well.

So, even though we were a nuclear family, but we never considered ourselves nuclear, in the sense that during school or college holidays, my uncles, the younger ones, all came to either our house, mostly our house, or another older brother who was married. This continued till most of them were married. For instance, my mother got the younger aunt married.

My father was the fourth brother so there was financial inter dependance. And I know that we went through a little bit of financial stress, because his younger siblings had to be looked after, sent to college, got married and all of that. Then later on their children, also joined in. We never felt this whole thing about my brother and my cousin brothers, there was really no distinction at all. My aunts and my uncles gave us the same affection that they gave to their children. It was all like, Oh, they're my own brothers and sisters.

Does your family come from government service, professional or family business?
We were a completely professional family. My paternal grandfather, he was an engineer in the public works department at that time, quite a high-ranking officer. And my mother's father was in the IAS. He was a district magistrate when he retired, he was also given Rai Bahadur award, but he refused to take it because it was given by the British.

What was the environment like at home? With so many boys – was it strict discipline / Laissez faire / Girls are = boys or any other?
My family was, though they were very loving and very open, there was a distinction between girls and boys. Boys were expected to get ahead in life.

My family is filled with engineers and doctors but the girls basically were not encouraged to pursue professional education. They were never stopped if they wanted to study further, but if they wanted to go and work, that was very much frowned upon. They were fundamentally conservative. My father and all my uncles, shared the same value systems and thought process. They had the same ideas. They were not that westernized in this respect.

But from my mother's side, they were more westernized. My grandfather used to work for the British, So, they were much more westernized, emancipated in the sense that the women were allowed to study as much as they wanted. He sent all his six daughters to university. But he also was also not very open to the women working. One of my aunts who started working, was a bit of a rebel. She said, I'm not going to get married now, I'm going to start working. My youngest aunt was a doctor. They were twins - one being a doctor, and other one was a teacher. Both worked. By that time my grandfather had come around to the point that he was more flexible. He was not hindering them from working, but definitely, in both the families the girls were expected to marry. That too as per the caste. That expecttaion never changed.

My father remained conservative. None of the girls really, except one cousin who was an architect, followed any professional education. After their education they were married off.

I started working after I got married. It was upon me; I was totally self- driven.

What were some of stories you were fed to justify the environment at home. Any incidents which had a lasting impact on self-confidence?
It was stated very clearly, it was not an impression. If I look back, I grew up influenced more by my mother's side than my father's side, because my grandfather had built a house in Calcutta and we used to go there for holidays. That was more

of a second home for us. I grew up with five boys. There was two years of difference between the five of us. We're very, very close, we played together. But even when we were small, roles were differentiated. The boys would do more adventurous things and play all kinds of games they will cook up which included fighting. One of my uncles joined the army in fact. But I would not be included in those fights. I used to play cricket and I had to beg them to include me in the cricket. I was also the youngest so I was asked to make the sandwiches for lunch while they played.

All the boys were allowed to go abroad and study. I wasn't, so that was a big blow to my expectations. Going abroad and studying without getting married was out of the question.

What was school life like? Who were you in school - The teacher's pet, the class bully or mouse or the back bencher?
Well, the family values were very, very clear - that we are professionals. We're not born with a silver spoon in our mouth. So, whatever we are going to be, we have to activate ourselves. We were told very clearly; you're not going to be blessed with a house and money so do whatever you want. There was a great deal of emphasis on education and studying. So one never had the luxury of being a backbencher. It was always, are you coming first? Or, why have you come third?

What about your brother?
My brother was 11 years younger to me. I was in college when he was in school. But he also faced the same kind of pressure, in fact more because he was a male child.

On one hand girls were expected to not do anything before marriage and on the other, the message was that whatever

you want to achieve you have to do yourself. So, do you think it shaped you differently from other girls?
I think so. Just growing up with boys opened my horizons, to be able to do other things.

While I do regret that my parents never sent me to business school, I never got a management degree. But then I got a BA degree and sat for my PhD. So their thing was you study as much as you want, we are not going to interfere, but we're not going to send you abroad. So before getting married, I told my husband-to-be that "listen, there will be a time when I will want to go abroad and study". This goal I always had in my mind.

So in that sense I was a bit of a rebel, but also very shy. So, I couldn't really express myself back then otherwise I would have tried to go abroad and study even then.

What about college? How did your choice of college happen?
My college was a disaster. My mother went to university, she got an MA degree in English literature. And then I had an elder cousin who was also pursuing English so there was kind of a path outlined for me. That after your Senior Cambridge you will also apply to the same college in Kolkata. and you will finish studying from there. Because I used to write very well, the expectation was that maybe after that you can study journalism. So there was a pact between my mother and me. But the universe had other plans for me.

During this time, because I was a science student and I was in Meerut, some of my school friends had applied to this college called Lady Irwin College in Delhi, which was a very prized college because girls who pass out of that college, are very prized in the marriage market. It was not my thing but because all these girls were applying so I said, well, maybe I will also apply.

I had also applied to a college in Kolkata, in deference to my mother's wishes. When I was applying in Kolkata, the Naxal period started. So my mother backed out and said, I don't want to leave you there as I would have had to stay in my grandfather's house and that would have caused her a lot of worry. So, she said, don't do anything over there, come back home (to Meerut) and sit at home for a year. She would say the most ridiculous thing. I said nothing doing, and just picked up that application form that I had and sent it off to Lady Irwin. They accepted me and I went off to Delhi.

Now the point is I was not at all interested in Home Science, not a bit. It was not my career choice at all. So that was when I became a backbencher. I didn't study at all. I got lots of boyfriends, I spent a lot of time in this course, not studying, but just waiting for the exams and not clear the exams.

What about your Masters? Was your thinking process more career oriented by then? Where did you acquire your professional education and training from?
I did my MSc in psychology from Kolkata, Jadavpur University.

I started becoming serious in my Master's, when I started studying more of psychology. It really interested me and I decided that would like to be a psychologist. So, I started following that path. After that, I did my B. Ed. Degree. Doing a job would have been very difficult, in that family. Marriage was a way of escaping this. So I got married, and got my first job as a teacher.

In 1986, I came to Bombay with my husband. By that time I had realized that teaching is boring, So I did a course in counselling. Xavier's had a six-month course on counselling which really attracted me. I decided I wanted to be a counselor, a therapist. I worked with very esteemed institutions during this phase - St. Mary's School, Cathedral School. I was counselor for all of Cathedral's 4 schools.

Mental health / abnormal psychology fascinated me.

My husband never had any problems with me working. I would have had problems if I had started doing corporate work, you know, but because I had studied a lot of psychology and child psychology also, I knew about latchkey children, and I didn't want my children to be that.

At that point of time lot of women had started working in full time jobs. So children who came from those families, where both parents were working used to carry their own latch keys for the house. They used to open their door and come in when neither of the parents were there. So they were called the latchkey children.

What happens to latchkey children after they come home, there are no parents there to see to their needs or something, maybe one help is there. And when both the parents come home both are equally tired. There's very little of parenting that goes on for those children.

So, I always left with the children and came back when the children came back. I did that for many years. I was sure I didn't want to leave my children alone.

When and how did you get into your Process Work?
Then in 1989, I did this workshop on Process Work. At that time, I was working with Spastics Society. I was in charge of their adult training department. I felt this was magic, you know, I'm seeing magic. Then I went to assist them in 1991 / 92. That's when I decided that this was something that I

would really like to take forward. From then onwards, I was going to Portland every year for two, three months each time. My mother and father gave me amazing support, because my children were small, and they used to come and baby sit for me while I could go away without any tension at all.

I studied for seven years, and got my Diploma in Process Work.

Tell us a bit about Process Work and what drove you deeper into it?

Well, when I started studying psychology, I thought that I had actually found my niche and was really interested in that field. I was always doing pioneering work in that, nobody else was really doing all these things. In fact, without really understanding or being acknowledged or being aware of it, I had always been a leader in my work.

Process work basically is a model of psychotherapy, which was started by Dr. Arnold Mindell. He is a Jungian analyst, and he had a very big dream about starting his own school. He called that process oriented psychology which was based on Jungian psychology. It was a school which trained therapists. When Dr. Arnold Mindell came to India, there was a very small network of psychologists, psychiatrists and very few counsellors.

And at that point of time, I was also doing some work with Spastics society. I got fascinated by what I saw happening. And then there was an intensive course that they invited me to attend. I wanted to leave my job and start studying process work more intensely, I had to apply for leave. I was at that time in Cathedral and asked the principal. He said, you are already overqualified where do you want to go and study and do what? I said, well, I do want to study and then he said,

I'm not going to give you any leave. So I quit my job and continued with my studying.

I went to Portland to attend that. I found that was actually what I wanted to do, to become a therapist and work one-on-one with people.

After my diploma I started practicing. That grew very well. I was doing work for schools as well as corporates, that is when I also started doing a lot of leadership training. Process Work gave me this wonderful opportunity to also be in therapy myself. That brought a lot of Self - Awareness of what was going on in my life. It gave me a lot of encouragement to do what I really believed in.

Along with process work, I was also doing ISABS (Indian Society for Applied Behavioral Science). I did some training in Gestalt therapy and NLP. It was an intense learning period. There were a few of us, who were in the forefront of knowing and doing all this.

Then in 1995-96 we held a very big conference in India on Conflict Resolution, in India; something that has never been attempted, a World Work seminar. That was when I started the Process Work Institute in India.

What was your vision about this work? Did it have any influence on your personality or your career opportunities?
Conflict Resolution basically is a part, of this module of process-oriented psychology. And that is a new addition to any school of psychology. Because usually, schools of psychology do not work with large groups. So this was a kind of a large group intervention, where the facilitators worked with anything between 250 to 350, international group of people and worked in areas that were either war zones or had experienced conflict, or were on the edge of experiencing conflict. So it was

a large group conflict resolution methodology that was only offered by Harrison O in his open space technology. After that also, large group interventions have not been used as a form of therapeutic facilitation.

I am trained in that, yes. If you study process work, you have to be trained in that it's a part of the model. We have used it all over the world, in international conferences.

This method of training facilitators and applying this methodology, started off as a 15-day program. The first one that I attended was in the United States, there was a lot of work done on interracial, and anti semitism and all of these structural oppression issues. We went to Bratislava, to Czechoslovakia just after it split into Czech and Slovakia; to Russia, Europe, other places where we were invited, for large group seminars.

What will be your advice to young women about to commence their career?
To start their career? That's a very generalized question. But if I look back at my life, which is very different because I was much, much older than most people nowadays, who start their career. They have access to career guidance in school. I used to be in charge of all these things during my school counselor phase. I used to think that if there was even 10% available to us, when we were in school and college, then it would have made such a big difference to our career.

Nowadays all parents want their children to be either engineers or doctors or architects or something similar, even though there are so many other, more interesting options. My advice would be that, get aptitude testing done. Instead of going and failing, and then trying to find the right thing to do, or trying to find the right job, which will give happiness, go through the testing, so that you rule out things that you wouldn't like to do.

For instance, my son, even though we come from a strong technical background. His father is an engineer, an IIT / IIM, my brother is an IIT / IIM, he decided that he didn't want to do that, he didn't want to do engineering. When my son passed class 12, I supported him completely, and then you know, we had to fight within the family to support him. In fact, my brother sat me down one day and said that I hope you know what you're doing, you're actually ruining his life, because the conviction was that unless you have this very, very professional degree, your children are not going to be successful. But I knew, because of my background in psychology, that if the child is intelligent, then the child would be able to do whatever they liked. And that's what happened with my son. I sent him off for his high school to the United World colleges. He was a gifted child; he is of a superior intelligence and then he got the scholarships and admission into colleges. Then he got to be a Rhodes Scholar and went to Oxford and his subject was economics. Because I was in the profession, I could guide him properly.

In many schools it is done free of cost. And then people from different professions are invited to come and talk to the children.

Did the India culture ever prove to be a hindrance to you? If so, when? If not, then what is your secret in handling it?
India culture actually helped me a lot. Whatever I was, I was very passionately Indian in my values. It's totally ingrained in me, we come from an extremely India based family, we have never tried to be anything else. Very few of our family have

immigrated to US. Most of us are here and we are all very, very Bengali. Bengali culture is very different and very, very rich. So, there was absolutely no attraction towards western life except perhaps we speak English a lot, but we are always trying to conserve whatever we can of the culture, even with my grandchildren.

But the patriarchal part, did that not hinder your career in any way?
That definitely hindered my career. For instance, from the job perspective, then definitely I would have picked up a different one. I was going to be a journalist which was accepted in the family; a teacher or something similar, because women have been teachers for a very long time. But if you are going into a corporate organization and do some work there? Then of course the safety factor comes into play. Going out into the world, you need to have all the required skills.

I didn't handle it very well, I was a rebel in the sense that I did as much as I could, but I wasn't somebody who would run away from home or something like that.

So, walking the path, but within boundaries. What was your path?
Let me talk about my corporate experiences. When I decided to be by myself, and had finished my diploma in process work, I went and lived in Portland for a year and a half by myself. So I think, in retrospect, that that was a very good grounding to what I was going to do next. That took away my fear of having to live by myself or travel by myself or you know, I was always doing these things by myself. I used to take layovers. I included a couple of cities and I would roam around there and then come home. So there's always this spirit in me that is a

little bit more adventurous. And that's the real test.

I think when I entered the corporate world, I took up a job and then faced a lot of conflict. I think corporate life is very, very complicated. And one has to learn the ropes, very carefully, because it's very easy to get lost. I think my family values kept me afloat.

Foremost was to be honest with myself. The amount of work that I've done on myself because of the different kinds of therapy I have studied, is immense. Therapy tells me not to play games with myself. And there was always an inner voice which was my father's. He would be in positions, where he could have made a lot of money, but we never saw him do that. Those kinds of things, were deeply ingrained.

There was also a big thing about safety. I always followed that.

Then boundaries you know, laying your own boundaries and knowing what you are trying to do. But I can't say that I never got into trouble or my life was never a mess. I learnt some hard lessons too.

How do you put across a viewpoint which you know is conflicting with that of a male dominated group?
Because of my education, and my training in conflict resolution. I have had some training, in that respect. When I joined the corporate world, in my first job, I was using that knowledge with the CEO. There was some amount of conflict in the organization. I would talk to him, as I would talk to the head of the department. I am not a very aggressive person, but, I'm pretty assertive myself. The CEO, who was a British chap would address the organization, and then he would look at me and say, Should I say that, and I would nod, I was basically coaching him through the speech.

The Head of HR too trusted me a lot. He used to go with what I used to say.

I think that I do not take people for a ride is very clear in my stance, in my appearance and what I to say. So, they both trusted me a lot, and we introduced a lot of initiatives, which could have failed, but because I could see that this is the way to do it, I would tell them and we would do meetings together and all of that. By the end when he was leaving, the CEO said that I'm going to leave a message with the organization that every CEO should have a psychologist in their team. I thought that was a great compliment.

By knowing how to look at human processes that are going on in the organization, that are not apparent to everybody, it is possible to negate conflict.

What do you think is the most ideal professional dress for women at the workplace?
I am a very conservative person around these things. I think there needs to be a code in every organization around dress and demeanor.

This is where I think women get manipulated and exploited, when they feel that they have to be attractive to the opposite sex. Now, in my opinion, and this is all my opinion, I may not be correct, but I think exposure is absolutely a no, no. And I think we always need to be aware of that. It may not be in the spirit of ME-TOO movement and all that, but in my head, there has to be some amount of reality check. I joined ME-TOO and I think that's very justified, but if you look at the Indian male psychology, you will know that they have been brought up to look at women as objects. Now, how will you turn around and blame them for that, because they are not consciously doing it. There is this systemic oppression;

it is called systemic sexism. All men are subjected to this.

You can still dress very beautifully, by not exposing. That is my statement, Okay. Please don't invite things that you wouldn't like, by contributing to it yourself, I used to tell the women in my organization.

I've also been a part of the sexual grievance section, redressal cells and all that. And I am always telling the women that listen, it's very, very okay, for you to dress in a certain way when you're not in a professional setting. But if you are going to do that in the workplace, then is work going to happen or something else is going to happen?

Marriage & Career or Marriage or Career? What are your views? Do you think one has to sacrifice their career for marriage? Does marriage have anything to do with feeling fulfilled in life?

I did a three-year project with women around this theme in a particular organization. Now, if you ask me personally, I think the institution of marriage is really outdated. It needs looking into. It is not made to accommodate women who are not into looking after the house or babies and making chapatis. This particular outdated institution really has to revamp itself before women think of fitting into it.

Personally, this is my personal opinion. I think marriage is a defunct institution. I don't think women and men need to get married at all, unless they want to have children. And if they want to have children, they have to be very, very serious about it, and give up some of their career aspirations in order to look after their children. That's a given. Roles can be exchanged. They can have House husbands; women can continue, depends on who's doing better in the career till the children need looking after. But having children and then saying oh no, I don't have time to look after them and all that and getting maids to look after them. I think you need to sit back and think what are you really doing.

Women are free to walk out, it's legally supported. The power dynamics has changed. A woman and a man needs to go into a marriage maybe as a contract for two to three years, and then see how it is figuring out.

But looking at the parental expectations, how to bring about that transition?
They have to get over this paradigm that we have, that when women get married, they have to have children. There is no need for this paradigm any more. Women don't have to get married. Okay, they don't have to travel with their husbands if they do get married. They don't have to worry about having babies because having children is a choice nowadays. And you can make very, very informed decisions about how you want to live your life. And men and women both can have children without getting married. So, what are we really talking about?

The reason I say that there is no need for women to get married is because neither is there a financial need, nor does a woman need a man to get a child. There is nothing preventing people from living in open relationships. So why shouldn't they? Why should there be anything called Marriage anymore? Only for the safety and support of children.

In my generation divorce was like a taboo. Now, it is happening in every third marriage or fourth marriage, right? The reason this is happening is because unfortunately, in the institution of marriage, not enough has changed. Roles haven't changed and the role of the husband and the wife, the mother, the father and the parents, nothing has changed but what has changed is the role identification. A woman is not financially dependent on her husband anymore. So she is not willing to take any kind of abuse or sexism.

Equal world for women in India is a long journey. Not even 50% of that journey has been achieved. What we're really talking about is the educated women, which are like maybe 5 to 10% of the population. The rest of the population, especially the rural population are not even educated. So women are being exploited, just like they were being exploited before.

What we need to do is we need to really dream, keep dreaming and keep, going at it and keep changing the kind of way we bring up our sons, keep changing the messages that we give the women, keep changing legislation around divorce and dowry and abuse and violence and all of that in order to bring about substantial change.

What in your opinion, is the common mistake made by working women?
Women want different things. You see the whole point is that women do have the role of making babies. Men can't do it. Then women get confused okay. It competes with education, career. The competition is very strong. Now suppose you go to a management college. Then from among your batchmates, one person has stopped growing in her career while other will continue growing financially and designation wise. Just because she took maternity leave. This is a competition that many women get into. They make this mistake of unplanned babies, then they get frustrated, because they think, why am I the only person who can make babies? Why can't men make babies? So, in some ways this whole culture takes away the feminine part of them. And that then becomes a huge problem in their life, because then they get very confused – running away from what makes them.

In all organizations, whether you like it or not there is a glass ceiling. Not only organizations, in all families, like if a child is sick, the child wants their mother, not their father. So, this is where women then think, okay, enough of career, I have to leave. And it's only because there's no balance in their thinking and planning.

Tell me something about you as a person - What motivates you? How do you renew yourself? What do you read? What are your hobbies? etc

If you're looking at MBTI classifications, I'm an INFP, Since I am an INFP, I am obviously very, very introverted. I actually am very introverted. I don't like hanging out and I don't like parties and I don't like to go but what I do like is, I have my own company, I like company of a few friends. And I love to read. I love to go and see performances – dance, music, movies, I like doing all these things. And I like to learn all the time.

How would you like to be remembered by your peers? Have you thought about it?

Yes, I have. I want to be remembered for the way I laugh. I laugh at the drop of a hat. And people remember me because of my laugh.

Looking back, is there anything you would like to change in your life?

No. Nothing because I believe life and the universe plan the life and whatever happens is going to happen. I don't think I have any control over how my life has panned out.

I am very content with how my life has gone. You know,

I have enjoyed every bit of it. I've enjoyed my freedom. I'm telling you in retrospect. I wouldn't change even one thing

Anything unfinished?
No. I have some learning unfinished, but even if I don't do it and I die, who can?

Signing off is there something more you would like to say to the women who are going to be reading this, the youngsters?
Only thing I would say in this is not only to the women but also to men and women is to be like water, to live your life like a river, because the river's way, and how does the river flow? The river flows and takes the shape of whatever comes in between it to go to the sea. It goes around the boulder falls over something, goes under something. Always, always, always.

Having said that whatever the universe gives me I will deal with it. Because whatever the universe is it will also give me the support to deal with it and there's always a learning.

"My take on Anuradha Deb

Leadership

Anuradha's interview has been an afterthought in the book. And I am glad for it. It's like looking back in a room after you have finished cleaning it, you look back and admire your handiwork. Yes, the room looks clean now, everything is in its proper place.

But looks aren't everything. Because despite having such a vast ocean of qualifications, experience and dedication, she still has to beat her drum herself. No flow of investment here, no PR Firms tripping over themselves to reward her, have her on their boards. A man at this age, with her body of experience would be a well-publicized brand name with his courses fully booked, months in advance.

That is what is at stake for India – loss of body of home-grown knowledge not coded and preserved.

Her upbringing

Her childhood is a typical Indian family example, on the cusp of the joint family / nuclear family classification. It shows the best of both – a motivated girl creating something of value out of a compromise. What a girl can do even without parental support, by sheer dint of her own determination and presence of mind. Girls of 21st century – take notes.

Women specific

Anuradha says "Equal world for women in India is a long journey. Not even 50% of that journey has been achieved. What we're really talking about is the educated women, which are maybe 5 to 10% of the population". While Deena & Sucheta see changes happening . But that is because Anuradha is talking about the role of married women in society and Deena and Sucheta are talking about the corporate Boardrooms. So, not necessarily that their burdens at home are decreasing.

My view is that organizations in India are happy paying lip service, doing band aid work, improving diversity ratios or doing POSH workshops which is like getting a pedicure to treat blood transfusion cases.

The point is, what are we, the educated women, who have clawed ourselves out of the morass, going to do about it?